CONTEXTUALIZATION

CONTEXTUALIZATION
A Theology of Gospel and Culture

Bruce J. Nicholls

REGENT COLLEGE PUBLISHING
Vancouver, British Columbia

To the faculty and students of the Sydney Missionary and Bible College, Croydon, N.S.W., Australia

Contextualization
Copyright © 1979 Bruce J. Nicholls

First published 1979 by InterVarsity Press (US) and the Paternoster Press (UK)

This edition published 2003 by
Regent College Publishing
5800 University Boulevard
Vancouver, British Columbia
V6T 2E4 Canada
www.regentpublishing.com

The author wishes to express his gratitude to the Sydney Missionary and Bible College where some of the material of this monograph was given in a special lectureship series March 1978; and to Miss Elizabeth Brattle for her patient typing and retyping of the original manuscript.

National Library of Canada Cataloguing in Publication Data

Nicholls, Bruce J.
    Contextualization: a theology of gospel and culture / Bruce J. Nicholls.

Includes bibliographical references.
ISBN 1-57383-052-6

    1. Christianity and culture. 2. Communication—Religious aspects—Christianity.
I. Title.

BR115.C8N43 2003   261   C2003-906265-1

1

Cultural and Supra-cultural Factors in the Communication of the Gospel

One of the crises of our age is the breakdown in communication. As the world becomes a global community, peoples of sharply differing cultures are forced to live together, share the same natural and human resources, and create culturally pluralistic communities. This brings tensions in cross-cultural communication, whether in the depressed ghettos of Chicago or in the multiracial communities struggling for identity and justice in London and Birmingham. The same is also true of Nairobi, Singapore and São Paulo.

Travel, education, mass media, commerce and politics highlight both the opportunities and difficulties of cross-cultural communication. For Christians committed to communicate a revealed and universal gospel to people in rapidly changing cultural situations, the task is acute. The difficulties are accentuated by the awareness that the messengers themselves are often the product of more than one culture. Third World missionaries, for example, need to understand at least four different cultures: the Bible's, that of the Western missionary who first brought the gospel, their own and that of the people to whom they take the gospel. Rapid advances in anthropology and sociology have helped to focus attention on the cultural factors in communication and to bring forth a flood of cultural theologies.

Signs of Cultural Insensitivity

Evangelical communicators have often underestimated the importance of cultural factors in communication. Some have been so concerned to preserve the purity of the gospel and its doctrinal formulations that they have been insensitive to the cultural thought patterns and behavior of those to whom they are proclaiming the gospel. Some have been unaware that terms such as *God, sin, Incarnation, salvation* and *heaven* convey different images in the minds of the hearer from those of the messenger.

Even those hearers who have had long contact with Christian missionaries or national Christians may continue to give a totally different interpretation to the gospel. For example, Mahatma Gandhi was a Hindu who had a long acquaintance with Christian missionaries and an extensive knowledge of Christian belief and practice. I have personally examined his Bible and noted how carefully he had underlined verses in the Sermon on the Mount (Mt. 5—7). Yet he could write, "I have not been able to see any difference between the Sermon on the Mount and the Bhagavad Gita. What the Sermon describes in a graphic manner, the Bhagavad Gita reduces to a scientific formula.... Today, supposing I was deprived of the Gita and forgot all its contents but had a copy of the Sermon, I should derive the same joy of it as I do from the Gita."[1]

Again, some Christians have been slow to reflect critically on the impact of their own cultural heritage and personal experiences on their understanding and interpretation of the gospel. They assume that it is possible to transmit the pure gospel of the Bible direct to the hearer without the carrier modifying it.[2] It has often been noted in India where missions have observed a strict territorial comity that there are sharp differences in the life and witness of churches in adjoining districts, reflecting the differences in the religious cultures of the founding missions.

Another sign of this insensitivity to cultural factors is the common case of the preacher who proclaims the gospel in virtually the same way to every audience whether they be Catholics, Hindus, Muslims or Marxists. Too often the hearer is treated as if he or she were a *tabula rasa* and the assumption made that because the gospel is the Word of God "it will not return to me void."

The fact that four cultures are usually involved in communicating the gospel is further complicated since many people today are the product of several cultures—traditional and modern, religious and secular. It is only in the last two decades that evangelicals have taken this situation seriously.

The recent Church Growth movement pioneered by Donald McGavran has through numerous case studies called for a new sensitivity to cultural factors that contribute to or hinder the growth of the church and the discipling of the nations. Why, for example, has the church in Korea grown from virtually no Christians at the turn of the century to fifteen per cent of the population with over 600,000 new additions every year, while in the neighboring country of Japan the total Christian community is approximately one per cent of the population? Why, for example, in India is Nagaland more than sixty per cent Christian while Rajasthan is only a tenth of one per cent Christian? To put the question another way: why do some people resist the gospel more than others?

The Willowbank Report of the Consultation on Gospel and Culture, Bermuda, 1978,[3] drew attention to two cultural barriers to effective communication of the gospel. "Sometimes people resist the Gospel," it states, "not because they think it false but because they perceive it is a threat to their culture, especially the fabric of their society, and their national and tribal solidarity."[4] The *Report* notes that to some degree this is unavoidable because Jesus Christ is a disturber as well as a peacemaker, and he demands total allegiance. The first century Jews certainly saw the gospel as a threat to their Hellenistic Judaism. The more sophisticated the culture the more likely is such a threat to be felt today. At the same time the *Report* observes, "There are features of every culture which are not incompatible with the Lordship of Christ, and which therefore need not be threatened nor discarded, but rather preserved and transformed." The capacity to perceive this distinction and to accept cultural factors which may be contrary to the messenger's own heritage, vary enormously from one mission agency of church to another.

The second barrier to communicating the gospel is that the gospel is often presented to people in alien cultural forms. The *Report* states, "Where missionaries bring with them foreign ways of thinking and behaviour, or attitudes of racial superiority, paternalism or preoccupation with material things, effective communication will be precluded."[5] This difficulty is not limited to the pioneer carrier of the gospel but is often perpetuated by the national church which, from a feeling of insecurity, seeks to preserve the status quo and so perpetuates the same cultural barriers. When these cultural mistakes are committed together, the problem is compounded. The image that Christianity is a foreign religion, a Western religion, a white man's religion, is one of the more serious handicaps to effective evangelism in Africa and Asia today. Islam in Africa has sought to foster this image of Christianity and to present its own image as a black man's religion which belongs to Africa.

The call to greater sensitivity in cross-cultural communication is a call to patience in understanding, to a humble pilgrimage of discipleship and a call to loving engagement with people in the realities of their daily life. It is to have the mind of Christ who renounced his glory and status, identified with people in their humanity and became a suffering servant even unto death.

Culture: A Design for Living

In the minds of many people the word *culture* is associated with activities such as drama, music, art, poetry, literature, and a cultured person is thought of as one who has acquired a sophisticated knowledge of these activities and who lives a life of refinement and good manners according to the ideals of society. This popular definition is too narrow for culture embraces the whole of life. In the words of Louis Luzbetak, "Culture is a design for living. It is a plan according to which society adapts itself to its social and ideational environment."[6] The term *culture* as such is an abstract concept. It must always be conceptualized as involvement in living. Professor John S. Mbiti at the Pan African Christian Leadership

Assembly, Nairobi, 1976, gave a working definition of culture as "the human pattern of life in response to man's environment"—expressed in physical forms such as agriculture, arts, technology; in inter-human relations such as institutions, laws, customs; and in forms of reflection on the total reality of life such as language, philosophy, religion, spiritual values, world view.[7]

Cultural behavior is not biologically transmitted from one generation to another. It must be learned by each succeeding generation. It is the sum total of the learned behavioral patterns and attitudes of a given community. The term *enculturation* is used for the process by which people learn the way of life of their society. This process takes place through direct and conscious instruction by parents, teachers or elders. It is learned by deliberate observation and imitation as when a child copies adults in everyday living. It is also learned through unconscious imitation and absorption. Because culture is acquired, it is constantly changing. It is relative. When the change is quicker than the community capacity to adapt to it, we may rightly speak of "culture shock."

G. Linwood Barney has given a helpful model of the arrangement of this acquired knowledge.[8] He suggests that each culture is a series of layers the deepest of which consists of ideology, cosmology and world view. A second layer which is closely related and probably derived from it is that of values. Stemming from both of these layers is a third layer of institutions such as marriage, law, education. These institutions are a bridge to the fourth and surface layer of material artifacts and observable behavior and customs. This surface is easily described and more easily changed. Each layer is more complex and abstract, and it is more difficult to define the functional relationships between them. Thus culture is a common integrative functional systematic whole, what Barney calls a "Shared Cognitive Orientation" of common knowledge. It will be noted that the levels broadly correspond to Mbiti's pattern of the physical, the interhuman and the reflection on the totality of life. All models have their limitations, and this one of a ladder of layers does not sufficiently show the interaction of each level with the others as a dynamically operating system. Perhaps a better model would be a sphere of which each segment is in proximity to the others or again of a pyramid with the world view as the unseen base, and values, institutions and observable behavior as the three sides each interacting with the other.

Religion, as a human factor in culture, influences and is influenced by each of these layers or segments. The dominating influence of religion in this plurality of segments is particularly evident in the religions of preliterate societies such as in animist cultures.[9] But it is equally fundamental to the great philosophical and ethical religions of Hinduism, Buddhism and Confucianism, and the prophetic religions of Judaism, Christianity and Islam.

In secular cultures, especially those that have a clearly defined ideology such as Marxism, the religious factor is either subsumed under others or is a focal point of reaction which gives coherence to the cultural behavior as a whole. It is significant that Marxism in Russia and in China has not been able to eliminate the spiritual factor of religion. There appears to be a rising tide of spirituality especially among the youth in Russia. In the case of China where traditional religious beliefs have been vigorously suppressed, the earlier cultural strand of obsession with astrology, palmistry and superstition about the spirit world appear to be reasserting themselves despite the continuing indoctrination of the political rulers along materialistic and mechanistic lines. The Christian assumption is that humans are spiritual and moral beings and that no self-conscious culture can suppress these factors indefinitely. In this sense culture is a macrocosm of spiritual man responding to his environment within the historical stream of his cultural continuity.

Any effective cross-cultural communication must take into account each of these factors. It involves the whole of humanity in the context of culture. Therefore if the gospel only modifies or changes a person or a community's observable behavior without producing an equivalent change in the fundamental world view, the level of communication is superficial. Similarly, to instill a new set of moral values in a society without noticeably producing changes in the institutions of that society is only a partial conversion.

The Importance of the Supra-cultural

Evangelicals take seriously the importance of the supra-cultural realm of reality in its interaction with human cultural factors. By supra-cultural we mean the phenomena of cultural belief and behavior that have their source outside of human culture. The reality of the spiritual realm of God and his kingdom and of Satan and his kingdom is an accepted assumption of the biblical writers. Apologetic arguments in defense of the existence of God and of Satan at best may confirm rather than prove their reality. In the last analysis belief in the supra-culture is a step of faith (Heb. 11:6).

The secular anthropologist and sociologist approach the study of culture from a different perspective. They assume that the world is a closed system and that all the factors of cultural formation, including the religious one, are contained within the system and determined by it, so that claims to knowledge of supra-cultural realms are themselves the product of the system.

The assumption of biblical Christianity is that God is the sovereign Creator and Lord who controls the created world and acts within it according to his own purpose. The biblical concepts of prophecy, miracles, eschatology and supremely the Incarnation point to the reality of this conviction. Therefore Mbiti's comment, "God gave us the Gospel. Man gives us culture,"[10] is not strictly true. The culture of the Hebrews was not just the product of their environment but was the interaction of the supra-cultural and the Hebrews in their environment and history. The Word of God changes the direction of culture and transforms it. The God of the Hebrews is also the God of the Christians and therefore the church, as the new covenanted people, is the sphere where change in culture is to be most expected.

It follows, therefore, that where Christ is truly Lord of his church the cultural design for living of its members will be different from those of the wider community. There will be a progressive movement toward a "Christian culture" which will reflect both the universality of the gospel and the particularity of the human environment. The lifestyle of the Indian Christian church, for example, will have distinctive qualities similar to those of any other national Christian church. It will manifest the fruit of the Spirit. At the same time it will be a truly Indian church divested of the world view, values and customs of Hinduism that are contrary to the gospel.

The boundary line between what is Indian and what is Hindu or Muslim is exceedingly difficult to draw. Only the lordship of Christ and the divine illumination of the Holy Spirit on the written Word of God can guide the believer and the church to make this distinction. Where there is no genuine interaction between the supra-cultural and national culture in the Christian community, it may be seriously doubted whether the kingdom of God is in any sense in their midst.

The other supra-cultural source of phenomena in culture is the *demonic*. Satan is a spiritual metaphysical reality whom John calls "the ruler of this world" (Jn. 12:31; 14:30; 16:11). And 1 John 5:19 states, "The whole world is in the power of the evil one." Paul takes this supra-cultural reality seriously. He speaks of Satan seducing the heathen to worship him (1 Cor. 10:20; 2 Cor. 6:16) and of the unbelievers being blinded by the god of this world (2 Cor. 4:4). Again, those who walk according to the course of this world follow "the prince of the power of the air" (Eph. 2:2). But his most frequent metaphor is of "principalities and powers" (Rom. 8:38-39; 1 Cor. 15:24, 26; Eph. 1:21; 3:10; 6:12; Col. 1:16; 2:10, 15). The reference in these passages to demonic cosmic powers is unmistakable.

The New Testament witnesses to the conviction that the world is not a closed system but the arena of a battle between the kingdom of God and the kingdom of Satan. It is both a battle in the supra-cultural heavenly places and in the world itself, a battle that was supremely manifest in the cross and in the resurrection of the incarnate Son of God. This battle is not an eternal dualism, for the decisive victory has already been won on the cross. Satan is dethroned and Christ is Lord, but this victory is still in the process of being actualized in human history and culture, and is moving to a culmination in the return of Christ in his glory to establish his reign on earth. This victory will be complete in the new earth and the new heaven. At that time the Antichrist, the incarnation of the evil one, will be destroyed. In the context of this final return and resurrection the hope will be realized that "then comes the end, when he delivers the kingdom to God the Father after destroying every rule and every authority and power. For he must reign until he has put all his enemies under his feet" (1 Cor. 15:24-25). The whole of creation will be liberated from its bondage to decay and obtain the glorious liberty of God's children (Rom. 8:19-22). A truly Christian culture will then be manifest.

The reality of the conflict between the supra-cultural and the cultural is all important in any adequate understanding of the issues of cross-cultural communication. Culture is never neutral. Every culture reflects this conflict. Religion is never purely a human affair, but an encounter within the supra-cultural realm of the kingdom of God and the kingdom of Satan. Mbiti infers that culture is neutral when he says, "so then each culture must count it a privilege to have the Gospel as its guest. African culture must extend its hospitality to the Gospel as an honoured guest that, hopefully, may stay for many centuries and millennia as the case may be."[11] This view does not give sufficient attention to the interaction between the supra-cultural and cultural. The gospel is never the guest of any culture; it is always its judge and redeemer.

Biblical Foundations for Our Response to the Gospel
The dynamics of culture as a design for living must be understood within the framework of a knowledge of the nature of humankind and of their relationship to the supernatural. For example, a Marxist view of humanity and history will predetermine the values and interpretation given to cultural behavior. This is equally true of a Hindu, Islamic or an animist view of human nature. The Christian lifestyle begins with a biblical world view of God, nature and people, and the Christian understanding of communication depends on it.

The dignity of man in God's image. A true knowledge of human nature depends upon a true knowledge of God. The Lausanne Covenant says, "Because man is God's creature, some of his culture is rich in beauty and goodness. Because he has fallen, all of it is tainted with sin and some of it is demonic. The Gospel does not presuppose the superiority of any culture to another, but evaluates all cultures according to its own criteria of truth and righteousness, and insists on moral absolutes in every culture" (para. 10).

The biblical view of culture is grounded in an understanding of the creation event as a fact that must be accepted and understood by faith (Heb. 11:3). The interpretation given to creation is always the fundamental watershed between cultures. In the biblical account of creation human beings are the image bearers of God both as individuals and as a corporate person. God created human beings as male and female so that in a real sense, as Karl Barth has noted, man and woman together constitute the image of God. This idea of corporate personality is found not only in the first Adam but in Jesus Christ, the new man who incorporates all believers in himself (Rom. 5:12-21). The last Adam is the heavenly man whose image the resurrected people of God will share (1 Cor. 15:45-49). Thus the Bible recognizes the priority of the individual but makes the social group of the family the basic unit of society.

From the calling of Abram to the letters of the New Testament, Israel, and later the church, are viewed from the standpoint of kinship and family. Most cultures recognize in varying degrees the institutional structure of the family as the basis of society. It is only in the secularism of Marxist culture that, at least in theory, the family is replaced by the larger social unit of the state.

The creation story affirms that God formed Adam of dust from the ground and gave to him a spiritual life which transcends the breath of the animal kingdom. The nature of human beings as a psychosomatic unity is emphasized so that in some sense man as body-soul is created in the image of God. Scripture has little interest in a disembodied spirit or soul, or in a soulless body. Each person is also capable of a depth of interpersonal relationships both with his or her maker and with his or her mate, a further aspect of the nature of the divine image (Gen. 1:26; 5:1; 9:6; 1 Cor. 11:7).

Throughout its history the church has struggled to understand the nature and meaning of this *imago Dei*. The early church and the Eastern Orthodox churches have usually stressed the ontic or essential content of the image of God in terms of the categories of reason, freedom, personality and so forth. Emil Brunner in his distinction between the formal and the material image comes near to the Orthodox view. On the other hand, the Reformers and evangelical theologians generally have stressed that the image of God is primarily a relational one. They recognize the uniqueness of human reason, freedom and personality but stress the relational continuity of knowledge, love, righteousness and holiness of the original image and of its renewal in Christ in the new humanity (Eph. 4:24; Col. 3:10). The continuity and discontinuity in these relationships is fundamental to a Christian view of culture.

The Christian view of people also affirms that God endowed them with the gift of creativity. God, who is the Creator, gave to people the gift of creating after his own image, not *ex nihilo* but out of the primary space-time created world. In creation God blessed man, male and female, and said to them, "Be fruitful and multiply, and fill the earth and subdue it" (Gen. 1:28). The first stage in this dominion over creation was in the naming of creation. God named each day of creation and empowered Adam to name each living creature (Gen. 2:19-20). Adam named the female, woman, thus declaring his headship of the human family (Gen. 2:23). The man's use of poetic language in naming the woman is the first evidence of the aesthetic expression of culture.

In Genesis 4:17-22 other elements of cultural behavior are described. The descendants of Cain built cities, kept livestock, made musical instruments and tools of bronze and iron. In the right use of these creative powers people glorified God, lived in harmony with their neighbors and so their culture reflects the richness of beauty and goodness.

The effect of the Fall and the knowledge of the gospel on human behavior. The personal and social implications of the Fall radically affected all people and all cultures. As Paul argues, "Therefore as sin came into the world through one man and death through sin, and so death spread to all men because all men sinned" (Rom. 5:12). In the Fall man rebelled against the lordship of the Creator, sought to assert his autonomy and disbelieved the law of God. The result was alienation from the Creator, a breakdown in harmony between the man and the woman, and deceit and violent death within the family. In aspiring to be like God, knowing good and evil, man became an idolater creating God in his own image, only to discover that he became a slave of the image which he created. His self-confidence and arrogance is seen in the building of the city and tower of Babel, which resulted in deep alienation at the most personal level of communication, that of language (Gen. 11:1-9).

Paul gives a detailed theological commentary on the Fall in his analysis of idolatry and the consequent judgment of God in wrath (Rom. 1:18-32). Because of the "total inclusiveness" of sin, all of culture "is tainted with sin and some of it is demonic." Thus every segment of culture—world view, values, institutions, artifacts and outward behavior—are perverted and abused.

It is against this background that the gospel is the good news of redemption both for each person in their individuality, in their social behavior and in their design for living. The gospel of redemption begins at the point of the Fall itself (Gen. 3:15) and reaches its culmination in the new Jerusalem coming down from heaven and the voice from the throne, "Behold, I make all things new" (Rev. 21:2, 5).

The focal point of this redemption is God becoming man, an Incarnation of such reality that it could only happen once in contrast to the repetitive character of incarnations in other religious cultures. The purpose of the Incarnation is the cross where once and for all God reconciled humanity to himself.

In the mystery of the resurrection redemption reaches its high point in an amazing unity of continuity and discontinuity between the material and the spiritual. The significance of the hope of the resurrection for cultural behavior is seen in comparing the Hindu concept of immortality or annihilation with the Christian's expression of it in the ceremonies of death and burial. The hope of the resurrection includes the total transformation of culture when the supra-cultural kingdom of God is established on earth and Christ is Lord of all of creation (Eph. 1:10; Col. 1:20). In this present age the church as the new community of the people of God is the visible manifestation of this new society to the extent that Christ is Lord. Thus the resurrection stands as the ultimate model of both the universality and the humanity of the final Christian culture.

The sovereignty of God in the communication of the gospel. The God of biblical revelation is not a deist God who passively awaits the final day. He is the God who loves the whole world and calls all men and women to himself in repentance and faith. He leaves no one without a knowledge of himself so that sin is always sin against a better knowledge and therefore all are without excuse (Rom. 1:20). Those who have never heard the gospel of Christ are not without a knowledge of God through his universal revelation, but because of the devastating effect of sin this knowledge of God brings judgment and not salvation. All people know they ought to love the Creator of the divine laws, but in their rebellion they become a law to themselves. Only in the sovereign grace of God drawing sinners to himself in repentance and in the gift of faith can those who have never heard of Christ be reconciled to their Creator.

The living God is ever speaking to all people, of which fact conscience is testimony (Rom. 2:14-15). People not only have a knowledge of God's "eternal power and deity" and the law "written on their hearts" but many cultures give evidence of a perverted knowledge of an atoning sacrifice for sin as the only way to reconciliation with God. It is of some significance that the Rig Vedas, the earliest of the Hindu scriptures, have glimmers of the truth of propitiation and expiation in their sacrificial system, overlaid with perverted concepts of appeasement. God in his sovereignty uses the human foolishness of cultural arrogance to prepare ethnic communities to hear and receive the gospel.

The awareness that God the Holy Spirit is the true messenger of the gospel who always goes before us, preparing people to hear and receive the gospel, causes us to cry out with Paul, "For necessity is laid upon me. Woe to me if I do not preach the gospel!" (1 Cor. 9:16).

2

Patterns in the Movement from Contextualization to Syncretism

Throughout the modern missionary movement the mission of the church has been framed in terms of indigenization. In the writings of Henry Venn, Rowland Allen, Melvin Hodges and others, the goal of indigenization is a church that is self-governing, self-supporting and self-propagating. Attempts to indigenize (to varying degrees) forms of worship, music, church architecture and patterns of evangelism have been both encouraged and discouraged by missionaries and their agencies. In a similar way the younger churches have responded both positively and negatively to their own cultural heritages.

The Indigenization-Contextualization Debate
Since the colonial era came to an end following World War 2, there has been increasing frustration with the nineteenth-century formulation of the indigenized church by the younger churches in their search for self-identity and their enthusiasm to participate in the national life of their new nations. The urban churches have felt the impact of the modern technological revolution and the drift to secularism. Independence has brought with it new social,

economic and political factors which are radically affecting the lifestyle of the people. The widening knowledge of anthropology and sociology has helped to create a new self-awareness and cultural sensitivity.

Early in 1972 a new word, *contextualization*, began to be used by Shoki Coe and Aharon Sapsezian, directors of the Theological Education Fund (TEF). The TEF report for that year, *Ministry and Context*, suggested that contextualization implies all that is involved in the familiar term indigenization, but seeks to press beyond it to take into account "the process of secularity, technology and the struggle for human justice which characterized the historical moment of nations in the Third World."[12] The report introduces the TEF's Third Mandate as a response to "the widespread crisis of faith and search for meaning in life; the urgent issues of human development and social justice; the dialectic between a universal technological civilization and local culture and religious situations."[13]

Contextuality, it is claimed, is the capacity to respond meaningfully to the gospel within the framework of one's own situation. Contextualization is not simply a fad or a catchword but a theological necessity demanded by the incarnational nature of the Word.

How necessary is it to replace indigenization by contextualization? James O. Buswell urges that we should think twice before rejecting indigenous, indigenity and indigenization.[14] He suggests that the word *indigenization*, which means "to bear or to produce within," is not a static concept. It is as future orientated as the people who use it. He thinks that it is particularly appropriate for the church as the point where Christianity is indigenous within a culture. The term is less abstract and technical than *context* and more symbolic and effective. It is more easily understood by ordinary people. In the end it is not so much the word used as the meaning that grows up around it that is important. Rather than new words being created, older terms should be given new meaning and their abuses removed.

The concerns of the advocates of contextualization are valid. As well as addressing the gospel to the traditional cultural values, we must take into account contemporary social, economic and political issues of class struggle, riches and poverty, bribery and corruption, power politics, privileges and oppression—all the factors that constitute society and the relationships between one community and another. Contextualization takes seriously the contemporary factors in cultural change. Al Krass illustrates this awareness vividly when he writes, "Indigenizing concerns traditional culture, the kind of thing you read about in *National Geographic*. Contextualizing, on the other hand, concerns more the kind of thing you read about in *Time*. It relates to the current history of the world's culture."[15] It would be untrue, however, to say that there was no awareness of those concerns before the birth of the new terminology five years ago, but there can be no doubt that they have been given a new prominence in the developing nations in the postcolonial era.

Contextualization is part of a wider theological debate. The shift from the issues of indigenization to those of contextualization is part of a much wider theological concern for understanding the function of the church in the world. During the last two decades the process of secularizing Christian theology has gained momentum. At the Uppsala General Assembly of the World Council of Churches, 1968, the concept of the unity of the church as a sign of the unity of mankind was introduced. At the Nairobi Assembly of the WCC, 1975, Philip Potter endorsed this goal when he said, "I want to keep always before our minds the fact that the ecumenical movement is concerned with the *oikoumene*, the whole human race as it struggles to discover what it means to be human in the purpose of God."[16]

Since Uppsala, mission as the history of salvation has progressively become the salvation of history and the world rather than of the church. The line between the church and world has become blurred. The Commission on World Mission and Evangelism's Salvation Today Conference, Bangkok 1972/73, focused on humanization described largely in social, economic and political terms. Great interest was shown in Chairman Mao as a contemporary savior. At Nairobi there was virtually no discussion on the Second Coming of Christ or on the ultimate spiritual destiny of humanity. Eschatology was very much realized in the contemporary secular world in terms of the struggle for liberation and the quest for human development.

In contrast to this trend the International Congress on World Evangelization, 1974, Lausanne, reaffirmed the church as God's agent in evangelism. The Covenant stated: "The church is the very center of God's cosmic purpose and is his appointed means of spreading the Gospel" (para. 6). And again, "Although reconciliation with man is not reconciliation with God, nor is social action evangelism, nor is political liberation salvation, nevertheless we affirm that evangelism and socio-political involvement are both part of our Christian duty" (para. 5).

Another aspect of the wider concern that focused at Nairobi was that of seeking community within the framework of the unity of mankind. World community was seen as the common search of people of various faiths, cultures and ideologies who seek to transcend the limitations of their own religious or local community. Combined with the concept of community was that of dialogue by which different communities learn to accept each other and to grow together toward the truth. The Chiang Mai, Thailand, consultation on "Dialogue with People of Living Faiths and Ideologies," April 1977, clarified many of the misunderstandings about dialogue and community, but in no way removed the apprehension of the few of us evangelicals present that world community presupposes an ultimate universalism and that dialogue can be pursued independent of evangelism and a call to conversion. It is now popular to speak of dialogical theory.

Evangelicals are equally concerned about the wider dimensions of the Christian faith because they are of biblical importance. Therefore, any discussion on the contextualizing of the gospel in terms of God's work in the world of economic and political structures cannot be separated from the work of evangelism and the indigenizing of the church. The contemporary issues in the contextualization debate and the traditional understanding of indigenization are both important for an evangelical theology of the gospel and culture.

An Evaluation of Models of Contextualizing Theology

Any critical analysis of contextualization ought to be global, but, for the purposes of this study, the patterns of contextualization will be largely limited to selected parts of the Third World. As a broad generalization, we may speak of two levels of contextualization— cultural and theological. The former relates primarily to the two surface levels or segments of culture as discussed in the first chapter, namely, the institutions of family, law, education and the observable level of cultural behavior and the use of artifacts. These tend to be the preoccupation of the anthropologist and sociologist whose approach is more phenomenological and concerned with ethno-theology.

On the other hand, the deeper levels of culture, namely, the world view and cosmology and the moral and ethical values that are derived from them, are the primary concern of the theologian. It is not surprising that these two groups are suspicious of each other for they speak different languages, approach culture from different perspectives and look for different sets of results. The Consultation on Gospel and Culture at Willowbank, Bermuda, January 1978, was an attempt to help evangelical theologians and anthropologists begin to talk and, more appropriately, to listen to each other.

Again, as a broad generalization, it may be helpful to speak of two approaches to contextualization: existential contextualization and dogmatic contextualization. The first assumes an existential approach to theologizing which is especially popular in ecumenical circles and most of the contemporary literature on contextualization is written from this point of view. The second approach begins with an authoritative biblical theology whose dogmatic understanding is contextualized in a given cultural situation. The two approaches are, of course, not irreconcilable alternatives, but the starting point for doing theology will determine the end product. Each approach to doing theology carries its own presuppositions and pre-understandings. In this chapter we will seek to give a critical evaluation of existential contextualization and in the following chapter examine the case for dogmatic contextualization.

Existential contextualization involves the interaction of two basic principles: the essential relativity of text and context, and the dialectical method of the search for truth. This is the presupposition of Western existential theology. It is now widely accepted that all theology, including biblical theology, is culturally conditioned and therefore in some sense relative. Theologizing is understood as a human fallible process, so that no theology is perfect or absolute.[17]

The failure of missionary communicators to recognize the degree of cultural conditioning of their own theology has been devastating to many Third World churches, creating a kind of Western theological imperialism and stifling the efforts of national Christians to theologize within their own culture. Unfortunately the imposition of Western theological systems is often perpetuated by the national theologians themselves. I remember the dismay I felt when a leader of one of the "indigenous" churches in Japan expressed his enthusiasm for translating a three-volume American systematic textbook into Japanese without any apparent desire to evaluate critically the highly culturized system itself.

Every attempt to make theology relevant to people in a given cultural context will of necessity be culturally conditioned, for theology that communicates is always missiological. This, however, must not be confused with the nature and function of the cultural conditioning in the biblical revelation, where the sovereignty of God is at work in a way that is unique. This is discussed in more detail below.

The approach of existential contextualization is to assume that text and context are culturally conditioned and relative to each other. This position usually rejects any understanding of propositional verbal revelation as objective and authoritative on the basis that knowledge is never free from subjectivity. It denies the possibility of a single biblical theology, but rather speaks of plural biblical theologies, each conditioned by the writer's own community of faith.[18]

Special reference may be made to two important attempts to do theology in the Third World on the basis of existential contextualization. One is by a European missionary who worked in the Cameroons in Africa and the other a national of Sri Lanka with a Tamil heritage. Both belong to more than one culture.

Daniel von Allmen of Switzerland was formerly a member of the Protestant Theological Faculty of Yaounde, Cameroons. His article, "The Birth of Theology,"[19] was an expanded reply to Dr. Byang Kato's attack on Christo-paganism in theological trends in Africa.[20] He argues that all theologies beginning with Pauline theology are the result of contextualization. There can be no final dogmatic theology, for theology is always changing. Following Bultmann he argues that the gospel is the living preaching of the church's faith and its reflection on the Christ Event—Christ crucified and risen again. Theology is reflection upon this living preaching.

In the spirit of Ernst Käsemann he sees many contextualizations of the "Event" in the early church. He argues that New Testament theology is contextualized in the cultural forms of Hellenistic Judaism which was influenced by "a dying and a rising god" of the mystery religions. In his letters Paul both corrects and adapts this Hellenized gospel and so establishes a model for the contextualization of theology in Africa and elsewhere. Contextualized theology is a process of correction and adaptation.

Von Allmen argues that theology begins in the experience of preaching and is expressed first in worship and not in doctrinal formulations.[21] The relationship of doctrine to faith and worship is also a matter of debate among evangelicals.[22]

A significant corollary of this dialectical approach is that there can be no Africanization or contextualization of an existing theology. Von Allmen argues: "Any authentic theology must start ever anew from the focal point of faith, which is the confession of the Lord Jesus Christ who died and was raised for us; and it must be built or rebuilt (whether in Africa or in Europe) in a way which is both faithful to the inner thrust of Christian revelation and also in harmony with the mentality of the person who formulates it."[23] Thus, the flowering of a truly African theology will presuppose a state of tabula rasa, stripped of existing and especially Western theologies. He urges Africans to become aware of the value of their culture "in its own right, and not only its relative value" if a true African theology is to be brought to birth.

In these statements von Allmen has almost absolutized local culture. He has ignored the continuity of apostolic succession of truth and experience, encultured throughout the history of the church. Rather than teach an existing theology, even a so-called New Testament theology, he suggests that the theological educator should give high priority to the study of the history of traditions in the early church to enable us "to uncover the forces that govern the making of that theology, in order that we in turn may be guided by the same dynamism as we set about creating a contemporary theology, whether it be in Africa or in Europe."[24] This approach may lead to reducing theology to a comparative study of different cultural Christian traditions.

For the second model we turn to S. Wesley Ariarajah, a minister of the Methodist Church of Sri Lanka. In an article "Towards a Theology of Dialogue"[25] he argues in a similar way for the contextualizing of a radical existential understanding of the Christian faith. Ariarajah believes that one of the sins of the past has been to "absolutize the Christian religion and theology, implying that the other religions were false."[26] He suggests that "all religions seek to tell their religious experience within the framework of a 'story' of the nature of the world, of man, of God and the destiny of life." No one story is more valid than the others. "All stories have no enduring value in themselves, except to give a framework within which the community celebrates its faith and experience."[27] The Judeo-Christian "creation-fall-redemption" story is no more valid than the Hindu story of karma, rebirth and the essential unity of man and God. He adds, "Anyone who approaches another with an *a priori* assumption that his story is 'the only true story' kills the dialogue before it begins."[28]

Thus, for Ariarajah, text and context have only relative value and the existential experience of faith is the dialectical interaction between the two. He accepts the Western critical view that there is not one Jesus in the New Testament but at least five, and that the New Testament materials can only be understood as "faith statements" of the writers.[29] All scriptures, including the Bible, are "confessional material and they reflect the faith and belief of the people who composed them at a given time."[30]

Ariarajah sets his contextualization in the context of religious universalism. All human beings, not just Christians, are "part of God's activity in the world and share a common future."[31] Thus, the center of God's activity is "the human community." There is nothing particular about the Christian community whose self-realization does not "exclude God's purposeful activity in and through other faiths." He affirms that salvation history is the history of the whole of humankind and that "human history is the arena of God's saving purpose." At best the Christian community is "the provisional, the sign community."[32]

In reacting against the "teutonic captivity" of Christian dogmatic theology, Ariarajah has made a radical Western existentialism the basis for doing theology in a Ceylonese context. This overreaction to Western theology is understandable when Christianity was so often identified with colonial imperialism and the Western missionary was insensitive to the cultural values of the converts. Choan-seng Song of Taiwan expresses the same deep feeling when he says, "Such dogmatism and militancy exhibited by missionary Christianity have made the Gospel of Jesus Christ appear to be negative and exclusive not only with regard to other religious beliefs but also to Asian cultural expressions as a whole. . . . It seems that the more dogmatic a Christian is, the better missionary or evangelist he would become."[33] One of the unfortunate results of this type of overreaction is the inability to distinguish between biblical theology and Western theology.

The Dynamics of Cultural and Theological Syncretism
The spate of books and articles from Africa, Asia and Latin America leaves one in no doubt that Third World theologies have arrived. For example, a recent symposium, What Asian Christians Are Thinking, opens with Dr. E. P. Nacpil's exposition of "The Critical Asian Principle" as a situational principle, a hermeneutical principle, a missiological principle and an educational principle.[34] In Africa there is a burst of creative thinking and publications flowing from the pens of such people as C. G. Baeta, John S. Mbiti, Bolaji Idowu, Harry Sawyerr, Kwesia Dickson and Dr. L. O. Sanneh. In Latin America creative thinkers include Rubena Alves,

Hugo Assmann, Emilio Castro, Orlando Costas, Gustavo Gutierrez, J. Miguez-Bonino and René Padilla.

Syncretism is the attempt to reconcile diverse or conflicting beliefs, or religious practices into a unified system. At the WCC Assembly at Nairobi M. M. Thomas sought to rescue the word when he spoke of a "Christ-centred syncretism." However, the Assembly Report clearly opposed all forms of syncretism, "incipient, nascent, or developed," despite the strong protests of a number of Indian and Filipino theologians who argued that Christianity itself was syncretistic. It is now generally accepted that the term should have a negative connotation.

The contemporary concern to contextualize the gospel in particular cultures has raised the problem of syncretism in a new way. It is discussed at every study conference that covers the theme of the gospel and culture. *The Willowbank Report* stated: "As the church seeks to express its life in local cultural forms, it soon has to face the problem of cultural elements that either are evil or have evil associations. How should the church react to these? Elements which are intrinsically false or evil clearly cannot be assimilated into Christianity without a lapse into syncretism. This is a danger for all churches in all cultures."[35] At Lausanne one of the theology study groups gave special attention to the problem.[36] Byang Kato endorsed the plea of George Peters to save the African churches from "Christo-paganism, which is a real threat to the future evangelical church on that continent."[37]

On one hand there is a need for bold and creative attempts to utilize cultural forms that can be baptized into Christ without denying the gospel. The Chiang Mai consultation, Dialogue in Community, rightly affirmed the need for a genuine "translation" of the Christian message in every time and place going beyond verbal translation of the message by expressing it in "artistic, dogmatic, liturgical and above all in relational terms which are appropriate to convey the authenticity of the message in ways authentically indigenous."[38] An unhealthy phobia of syncretism can cripple true indigenization and contextualization.

On the other hand, the dangers of compromising the authenticity of the Christian faith and life are real as is seen in the early church's struggle with gnosticism and later in the compromising of the gospel in the so-called "civil religions" of the West. The message of Chiang Mai was summed up in the story of the little Thai lizards which climb the house walls and whose cries are interpreted as "Welcome" to the ventures of exploratory faith and "Take care" of the danger of syncretism.[39]

Syncretism as a dynamic principle may be intentional or it may be an unconscious movement of assimilation. Mithraism and Manichaeism in the early church attempted to assimilate the Christian faith. Theosophy, the Ramakrishna Mission, the Bahai Faith, are modern self-conscious attempts at synthesis. Kato refers to the seeds of syncretism being sown in the departments of comparative religion in universities in Africa. The cover design of Orita (a Yoruba word meaning a junction), the name of the Journal of Religious Studies, Ibadan, Nigeria, symbolizes Christianity, Islam and African traditional religion as having a common center.[40]

Throughout the history of Western Christian theology the truth of the gospel has suffered from an unconscious assimilation of conflicting tenets and practices. Augustine was unable to completely free himself from neo-platonism. Aquinas synthesized biblical faith and Aristotelian philosophy. Modern liberal theology in the West has been deeply influenced by the philosophies of the Enlightenment, evolutionary science and existentialism, and in the East by the philosophies of Hinduism and Buddhism.

In the contemporary debate on gospel and culture there are two types of syncretistic dangers—one cultural and the other theological. The anthropologists are the more sensitive to the first and the theologians to the second.

Cultural syncretism takes two forms. It may result from an enthusiastic attempt to translate the Christian faith by uncritically using the symbols and religious practices of the receptor culture, resulting in a fusion of Christian and pagan beliefs and practices. This is evident in Latin America where the Roman Catholic Church, since the conquest by the Spanish in the sixteenth century, has accommodated native animistic and superstitious practices into their Catholic ritual. A contemporary example of cultural syncretism is the unconscious identification of biblical Christianity with "the American way of life." This form of syncretism is often found in both Western and Third World, middle-class, suburban, conservative, evangelical congregations who seem unaware that their lifestyle has more affinity to the consumer principles of capitalistic society than to the realities of the New Testament, and whose enthusiasm for evangelism and overseas missions is used to justify noninvolvement in the problems of race, poverty and oppression in the church's neighborhood.

The second form of cultural syncretism is more aggressive and self-conscious. It is the spirit of the Pharisees and Judaizers who sought to force their cultural forms of religious conviction on their converts. Its modern form is often seen in mission or denominationally founded churches, as enforced ecclesiastical structures, or in social standards of right conduct and worldliness totally alien to the local culture. In the eyes of non-Christian neighbors, Christianity carries the image of a foreign religion.

Theological syncretism goes to the very heart of culture for it is the joining together of concepts and images at the depths of world view and cosmology, and of moral and ethical values. It is more destructive than cultural syncretism though in fact it usually leads to cultural syncretism of the accommodation type. It is more reflective than cultural syncretism. It relativizes the nature of truth and of epistemology, carrying the assumption that all forms of particular truths and practices are only expressions of universal and Absolute Truth. This type of syncretism is generally the concern of the theologian and the philosopher.[41]

The process of theological syncretism normally takes place on the basis of the combination of recognizable laws or principles. It begins by denying the finality of revelation as recorded in the Bible in terms of its historical and verbalized truth. It assumes that since all theology is culturally conditioned, it is not possible to know with assurance what is the Word that God has revealed. It confuses the supra-cultural with the cultural. It reduces all theology to the storytelling of one's experience and faith. Scripture is not "a dividing wall" which limits theological reflection and divides one community from another, but consists of "lampposts that shed light and illumination on the religious experience of the community."[42]

No one scripture is more valid or true than another. Ariarajah sees "no reason why the Hindu scriptures should not be meaningful and provide the context of faith in Jesus Christ for an Indian Christian." Scripture, traditions and experience are equally criteria of truth. Unfortunately this type of radical syncretism is more widespread in Asia than is generally known and constitutes a serious threat to evangelism and to church growth.

A second element in this dynamic theological process is the principle of universalizing the particulars of the Christian faith. It is the principle of reductionism. It attempts to regress from historical fact to ideal or timeless truths. The Jesus of history becomes the ideal cosmic Christ.

Gandhi, for example, universalized the historical particulars of Jesus Christ and reduced history to an idea. He declared that he had little interest in a historical Jesus. For him the Sermon on the Mount would still be true if Jesus was no more than a figment of the writer's imagination. However, assuming that Jesus was historical, Gandhi was able to write, "God did not bear the cross only nineteen hundred years ago, but he bears it today, and he dies and is resurrected from day to day. It would be poor comfort to the world if it had to depend upon a historical God who died 2,000 years ago. Do not preach the God of history, but show him as he lives today through you."[43] He rejected the possibility of a bodily resurrection of Jesus Christ on the grounds that the laws of nature are "changeless, unchangeable and there are no miracles in the sense of infringement or interruption of Nature's laws."[44]

The same principle applies to the reduction of the personal to the impersonal, so that God as personal and moral is a lower form of reality than the Absolute. The search to interpret the Christian God in terms of Shankara's Absolute has appealed to some Indian Christian theologians, particularly Roman Catholics. Raymond Panikkar's exegesis of the opening verse of the Brahma Sutra is a scholarly attempt to make this link.[45] The attempt to show the interlocking relationship between the Personal and the All and bridge the gap between the Creator and the creature in the pan-en-theistic theologies of Teilhard de Chardin and J. A. T. Robinson reflect a similar syncretistic spirit.

A third principle in theological syncretism is the principle of complementarity in which the sum total of particular truths is greater than the expression of any one truth. Truth is to be found in the consensus or synthesis of particular truths. In the contemporary search for the unity of mankind and in the dialogue between religions this principle has a particular appeal.

For example, in interpreting the nature of the human predicament attempts are made to accept its description in different religious traditions as complementing each other. Ariarajah argues that it is willful blindness to insist that the "creation-fall-redemption" story is the only true description of the human predicament. He sees the *advaita* description of the human predicament as *avidya* (ignorance), the *Saive Siddhanta* concept of *anayam* (the egoistic power of individuation) and the Buddhist understanding of *anicca, anatta* and *dukkha* (conditional change, nonchange and change as the source of pain and anxiety), as all providing meaningful theological frameworks in which to express the Christian concept of alienation.

While it is true that Hinduism and Buddhism do provide valid insight into aspects of the human predicament, in no sense can they be equated with the biblical view of sin because they do not begin with the biblical doctrine of God. Ultimately, this principle of complementarity leads to universalism in salvation and ethics.

A second example is Harry Sawyerr's attempt to show that the Genesis 3 account of sin falls short of the African situation where, for example, the Ashanti, Yoruba and Mende tribal myths interpret sin as violation of the harmony of society.[46] While this analysis may be an accurate description of alienation within tribal society, it is also an inadequate and partial explanation of the biblical understanding of sin.

A fourth principle is the principle of progressive absorption whereby all claims to supra-cultural uniqueness and finality are absorbed by naturalistic and humanistic ideas and practices. Divine grace is absorbed by natural law. To use Francis Schaeffer's model nature "eats up" grace. Syncretism is normative religion for fallen humanity. All claims to an authoritative Scripture, a unique Incarnation, a particular salvation are progressively absorbed in cultural relativism.

In a synthesis of Christian faith and other faiths the biblical message is progressively replaced by non-Christian assumptions and dogmas, and the Christian expressions of the religious life of worship, witness and ethics increasingly conform to those of the non-Christian partner in dialogue. In the end, the Christian mission is reduced to a so-called "Christian presence" and at best to a humanistic social concern. Syncretism results in the slow death of the church and the end of evangelism.

Three Models of Theological Syncretism in India

In any survey of the recent development of Indian Christian theology, the theological insights of Brahmabandhab Upadhyaya, A. J. Appasamy and P. Chenchiah are among the most frequently quoted case studies of theological contextualization.[47] The significant contribution that each has made to our understanding of the Indian cultural predicament and their insights into aspects of biblical truths are ably described by these and other writers. The limited concern of this chapter is to show the common pattern of their movement from indigenization and contextualization toward syncretism.

Brahmabandhab Upadhyaya (1861-1907), a Hindu convert to Roman Catholic Christianity, pioneered the use of Shankara as a philosophical instrument for the exposition of Christian theology which he interpreted within a Thomistic framework. He sought to indigenize pure Christianity in terms of pure Hindu vedic culture using the nondual monistic categories of *advaita vedanta* which he believed represented the highest point of Hinduism. He sought to equate God as "pure being" with *Brahman* described as *Sat, Cit* and *Anand* (being, intelligence and bliss). In relating the Christian Trinity to these concepts he believed he was preserving a higher conception of God than is possible on a personalistic interpretation. He went on to interpret the Incarnation in terms of Vishnu, God manifest, rather than in terms of Krishna an *avatar* who, as contingent and finite, belongs to the realm of *maya* (illusion) and the created world.

Upadhyaya's theology is an exercise in natural theology. His writings trace a progression in which his natural theology absorbed his revealed theology. For example, atonement became a vicarious transference of suffering by mystical identification after the pattern of the Hindu god Shiva, the manifest of the unmanifest Brahman. Robin Boyd suggests that his significance lay in his pioneering attempt to isolate cultural Hinduism from religious Hinduism and to merge cultural Hinduism with the Christian tradition.[48] However valid this insight might be the practical outcome of his natural theology was a syncretistic religious experience in which he increasingly accepted Hindu ritualistic customs, including the worship of Hindu gods as *avatar*, and upon his untimely death was cremated according to Hindu rites. By the end of his life he had no doctrine of the church and no interest in evangelism.

A. J. Appasamy (1891-1975) in his early years attempted to "appropriate the spirit of the best that India had to offer" in terms of the philosophical tradition of *vishishta advaita* of Ramanuja in whose semipersonalistic philosophy he found a key to the mysticism of the fourth Gospel. In order to interpret John's Gospel as *bhakti marga* (the way of devotion and love) he was forced to a reductionist process in his interpretation of the relationship of the Father to the Son, of sin in relation to *karma* and a virtual universalism in salvation. There was little room in his system for resurrection or grace. He had few references to the Holy Spirit. Appasamy's education was largely in the tradition of liberal scholarship and Neo-Platonistic philosophy. However, as a committed churchman and finally as a Bishop of the Church of South India, his theology became increasingly conservative and biblical and he became well known for his evangelistic work. His theological pilgrimage[49] is a significant example of a theologian who reversed the drift from indigenization to syncretism as he became more involved in evangelism and pastoral care.

P. Chenchiah (1886-1959) was born into a Hindu family and baptized at the age of fifteen along with his father. He became a successful lawyer and served for some years as a judge in an independent Indian state. He reacted sharply against Kraemer's *The Christian Message in a Non-Christian World* and with others published the famous volume *Rethinking Christianity in India* just prior to the IMC Conference at Tambaram, Madras, in 1938. He was attracted to the gnosticism of Sri Aurobindo and the naturalistic sciences of the West. From Aurobindo he learned the principle of integration by which lower levels of consciousness are sublimated into higher levels, and from the emergent evolution of Henri Bergson he learned the evolution of spirit as a pure flow of life-force in the world. Chenchiah had a single-minded devotion to Christ yet in the end it was an Arian Christ that he worshiped. He rejected the cross as an atoning sacrifice and thought of evangelism as reproducing or "becoming" Christ in humanity's upward evolutionary path. Despite his creative understanding of the *yoga* of the spirit and Christ as the new man,[50] he had no doctrine of the church and little interest in evangelism as traditionally understood. It would not be untrue to say that in the end his theology was a Hinduized Christian theology rather than an Indian Christian theology.

Dr. Saphir P. Athyal reminded the participants at the Bermuda Gospel and Culture consultation that Sadhu Sundar Singh's famous illustration, "the water of life in an Indian cup," is not as simple as it appears. He suggested the symbol of rice which when planted dies and then breaks forth from the ground as entirely new yet faithful to that which was originally planted. The gospel when planted in another culture, springs up faithful to its unchanging nature but rooted in its new cultural soil.

3

Understanding
Biblical
Theology

A central issue in today's theological debate is how we use the Bible. This issue of course has been central to every age of the Christian church but it is now particularly so because of developments in critical biblical studies, the new insights gained from the social sciences of cultural anthropology and sociology, the impact of technology and political theory in rapid cultural change and the issues raised by cross-cultural communication on a global scale. How we use the Bible will depend on our understanding of the nature of the authority of the Bible and on our understanding of the hermeneutical task in our approach to contextualization.

The Authority of the Bible in
Contemporary Ecumenical Movements
The Nairobi Assembly, 1975, was a crisis of faith for the WCC.[51] The founders of the WCC believed that the Bible was normative for their message to the world and the "biblical theology" school dominated by Karl Barth reached a high-water mark at the New Delhi Assembly in 1961, where the phrase "according to the Scriptures" was added to the doctrinal statement of the movement.

However, the fourth conference of the Faith and Order Commission at Montreal, 1963, proved to be a new turning point in the ecumenical movement's understanding of Scripture. Here the unity of New Testament ecclesiology was questioned and the hermeneutical problem of the relevance of the biblical message to the modern world was seriously raised.

These questions were further explored and a study on the "Authority of the Bible" was recommended by the Faith and Order meeting in Bristol in 1967. Ten regional study groups studied in detail different elements of the problem. The final report, representing a consensus of the groups, was approved by the Faith and Order Commission at Louvain, Belgium, 1971. This statement has become the working document of the ecumenical movement.

Evangelicals have always held the Bible to be normative and the final authority in all matters of faith and conduct. In the context of the assertions of critical scholars, evangelicals have been concerned about the nature of the process of inscripturation and such issues as infallibility and inerrancy. The Lausanne Covenant's statement on the authority and the power of the Bible has been widely accepted, but for some evangelicals it did not go far enough. The pressing issue now is one of hermeneutics and questions raised by the cultural conditioning of our theological understanding.

It is widely assumed among scholars that all theology is culturally conditioned. This statement needs careful evaluation. While it is true that attempts to contextualize theology by theologians both of the old and younger churches have been conditioned by a wide range of cultural factors, the crucial question remains: in what way and to what extent is the message of the Bible itself conditioned by the cultural setting of its authors? To what extent is the biblical message trans-cultural and how can this "gospel core" be clearly identified and objectified? What was the nature of God's control over these culturally conditioning factors in the inspiration of the writing of the Scriptures?

These issues surfaced in the Lausanne Committee's Consultation on Gospel and Culture, Bermuda, 1978. One focal issue of the debate was whether or not it was correct to talk of "the biblical theology" or is it better to speak of plural "biblical theologies"? This issue has far-reaching effects on our approach to the contextualizing of the gospel, the process of "doing theology" in a culturally pluralistic world.

Understanding our pre-understandings. It is essential to distinguish between our pre-understanding or prior assumptions and life-relationships of the nature of the Bible's authority and our pre-understanding of our own culture and the cultures of those to whom we communicate the gospel. The former is an attempt to understand biblical and dogmatic theology, which is the concern of this chapter, and the latter is the contextualizing of theology which is the concern of the following chapter.

Rudolf Bultmann has argued that there is no pure gospel and no neutral or presuppositionless exegesis, so that the hermeneutical task is a circular one with constant interaction between object and subject, text and interpreter. It is a dialectical process in which there can be no finality, only an approximation to the truth of the Word of God in a particular culture or situation. Bultmann has drawn attention to the interpreter's pre-understanding as the critical factor in this process. Pre-understanding is essentially a pre-commitment to the way in which the gospel is to be interpreted for a given culture. *The Louvain Report* recognized some sharp differences in the traditional and in the contemporary ecumenical understanding of pre-commitment to the authority of the Bible and its use. It describes the pre-understanding of the traditional (evangelical) approach as authoritarian, dogmatic and legalistic, using the Bible as a standard or norm for every problem and situation.[52] The Bible's authority is from outside our experience. It is an inspired book whose authority rests on the fact of its inspiration.

On the other hand the consensus of *The Louvain Report* reveals a different pre-understanding of the Bible. It states that by the authority of the Bible "we mean that it makes the Word of God audible and is therefore able to lead men to faith."[53] This authority is a subjective authority experienced when people hear God speak to them. One of the study groups thought it more appropriate to speak of the "role," the "influence" or the "function" of Scripture rather than its authority. Yet at the same time the Bible has a supra-individual character of authority as "the document of the faith of the Church."[54] It is not clear how these two concepts are related. The *Report* argues that historical criticism has shown the diversity of the biblical witness and that the events recorded are never "bare facts" but "always accessible to us in the clothing of their interpretation by the biblical authors."[55] Thus every interpretation is tied to a particular historically conditioned situation, some of which have greater importance than others. In a similar way, contemporary interpretations are determined by their own situation and must be seen as "the prolongation of the interpretive process which is recognized in the Bible." Thus, "situation-conditioned hermeneutic perspectives are inescapable."[56]

In rejecting the traditional doctrine of inspiration the *Report* defines inspiration in terms of the inspiring character of actual encounters with God. This raised the question as to why this should only be true of the Bible. The *Report* asks, "Why should not Basil, Augustine, Thomas, Luther or some modern author be inspired too? Surely it was their work of interpretation that led to the Bible's speaking once again with fresh authority."[57] The conclusion is that there is no hard and fast dividing line between canonical and noncanonical writings. The boundary is a fluid one.

The Formation of Our Pre-understandings

There are three factors that determine the interpreter's pre-understanding. First, there are ideological factors reflecting the interpreter's world view and system of values. Second, there are cultural factors that reflect the influence of the institutions and customs of society—legal, educational, economic and political systems. Third, there is the interaction with the supra-cultural, which may override all others.

The *supra-cultural factor* is either conversion to Christ and the acceptance by faith of his lordship over creation and history, or rejection of Christ in favor of secular humanism or Marxist atheism, or a turning to other religious gods, principalities and powers. For example, Mahatma Gandhi, though deeply influenced by the gospel, never accepted the lordship of Christ, and therefore his use of the Bible was always from the perspective of a Hindu monistic world view. This led him to a pre-understanding that Truth is God. The Muslim's pre-understanding of the nature of his encounter with Allah inevitably leads him to reject the possibility of the Incarnation and the cross. The Buddhist pre-understanding of the nature of the human predicament determines his interpretation of the nature of salvation, and so on.

A radical conversion to Christ produces a radically new hermeneutic. Paul's radical Damascus road experience totally changed his understanding of the Old Testament. Luther's conversion gave him a totally new perspective of the meaning of justification by faith. The reality of the Holy Spirit's impact on a person's life is a supra-cultural factor that modifies all others.

Evangelicals now recognize the importance of *cultural factors* in pre-understanding. Andrew Kirk refers to three such factors: the signs of the times, the social questions of injustice and oppression, and attitudes to evangelism.[58] It is idealistic to suggest that the Asian, African or Latin-American Christian theologian can free himself from all Western interpretation and begin again on the basis of his own culture. The cultural factors are too interrelated for this.

The Asian theologians that I know have all, like the missionary, been influenced by a plurality of cultural factors. They have been influenced by the traditional religious cultures of their country— Hindu, Buddhist, Islamic or animist. They are being influenced by secular materialism of the West. Their own Christian and ecclesiastical heritage, the economic and social status of their families, the politics of their local community, their secular and in particular, their theological education, especially at the graduate level, have all been important factors in the formulation of the prior questions and attitudes with which they approach the Bible.

Ideological factors obviously play a major role in determining our pre-understanding of the nature of the Bible's authority and the way to use it. Reference has already been made to a number of Asian theologians—Ariarajah, Upadhyaya, Appasamy and Chenchiah, whose understanding of the Bible has been significantly determined by their distinctive ideological positions.

A brief survey of the distinctive pre-understandings of some contemporary Western theologians who have had a profound influence on the formation of the pre-understandings of Third World theologians will enable us to see the complexity of the modern hermeneutical problems.

Rudolf Bultmann's pre-understanding of the cultural conditioning of theology goes back to the influence upon him of the relativizing theologies of the era of Adolf von Harnack and ultimately to that of Friedrich Schleiermacher. In asking questions about the human predicament, Bultmann draws his inspiration from Immanuel Kant, Sören Kierkegaard and Martin Heidegger (for whom language itself is interpretation). He conceives of the Word of God as an existential summons to live in openness to the future. His acceptance of a mechanistic scientific world view precludes any meaningful recognition of the supra-cultural elements in the biblical story. Bultmann demythologizes the myths of the New Testament to a nondogmatic gospel core, which he then attempts to reinterpret for the modern world in terms of his own pre-understanding of the human predicament. The new hermeneutic of Ernst Fuchs and Gerhard Ebeling only takes the work of Bultmann a stage further in a subjectively determined use of New Testament language and theology.[59] Their one-sided hermeneutic which virtually ignores the place of rational argument and statement has deeply influenced contemporary Third World theologies.

Karl Barth's pre-understanding of existential philosophy influenced his "Christological" hermeneutic by which he tested every passage of Scripture. This "christomonism," to use Paul Althaus's descriptive term, forced Barth to doubtful exegesis of passages to which the Christological test could not be applied. In contrast Alan Richardson of the British Biblical Theology School, so emphasized revelation as historical event that the hermeneutical task is restricted to a study of the Bible as recital and confession. Wolfhart Pannenberg begins with revelation as verifiable history open to all, but realized in the Christ Event. He rejects the sharp distinction between event and interpretation and sees every event as a Spirit-direct event.

The reduction of revelation to interpreted event and the limitation of faith to faith upon historical knowledge, eliminates from the category "Word of God" any understanding of a verbal and propositional element in divine revelation. Scripture in its totality no longer has a normative value and the content of faith is left undefined. We are grateful for the emphasis of the new hermeneutics on the role of the interpreters own experience of life on his exegetical and expository task, but a corrective and balance is needed. This leads us to a fresh understanding of our evangelical theological task.

Reforming the Evangelicals' Own Pre-understanding

Each of the pre-understandings so far described have a common emphasis on a subjective basis for acknowledging the authority of Scripture and in varying ways resort to reductionist methods to determine the Word of God. Their consequent theologies are reflections on their own encounter with God and their attempt to make this experience relevant to others. The evangelical's acknowledged pre-understanding assumes that the Bible has a unique God-given authority which transcends our experiencing of it.

The Lausanne Covenant states: "We affirm the divine inspiration, truthfulness and authority of both Old and New Testament Scriptures in their entirety as the only written Word of God, without error in all that it affirms, and the only infallible rule of faith and practice" (para. 2). The doctrinal statement of the World Evangelical Fellowship, which goes back to the World Evangelical Alliance of 1846, makes a similar affirmation, as do the statements of evangelical churches and parachurch organizations worldwide, irrespective of their own cultures.

While the use of certain phrases such as *infallible, inerrant, autograph,* can be traced to certain historical factors in the Western church, evangelicals believe that behind them stand supra-cultural verities which are inherent in the Word of God itself. Warfield and succeeding scholars have demonstrated the rationality of the Bible's testimony to its own inspiration and authority and the definitive teaching and example of our Lord in the use of the Old Testament. In the spirit of Augustine, evangelicals affirm, "What Scripture says God says." Evangelicals accept the Bible's self-understanding of the Word of God as interpreted event, as prophetic verbal word, dogmatic teaching, eschatological pronouncements and pre-eminently as the person of Christ and his work. The Bible's authority is derived from Christ's authority.

The critical issue in the evangelical's pre-understanding is his understanding of the inspiration of Scripture. James Packer has described it as "an activity whereby God, who in His providence overrules all human utterance, causes certain particular men to speak and write in such a way that their utterance was and remains, His utterance through them, establishing norms of faith and practice."[60] Evangelicals recognize that this pre-understanding is an act of faith consequent to the acceptance of Christ as Lord, but also that it is a reasonable faith for critical scholarship, rather than disproving with assured certainty the theological and factual claims of the biblical text, has increasingly resolved discrepancies and difficulties that would refute biblical infallibility. At the same time evangelicals do not ignore the unresolved critical issues and are careful not to impose a concept of inerrancy on the text that goes beyond the kind of inerrancy that the Bible teaches of itself.

A number of important points follow from this prior understanding. The unique inspiration of the canonical books, which God caused the church to recognize as such, ensures the essential unity and rationality of the biblical message. It is therefore right to speak of a unitary or undivided biblical theology. Recognizing the distinctives of the biblical writers' cultural heritage and situation, it is also correct to speak of Pauline theology, Johannine theology and so forth and to see these as authentic elements of the one biblical theology and that their "relational centers" are held together in a divine harmony. The Bible's theological pluralism is a pluralism of complementarity within a single divinely controlled whole.

The limitations of the interpreter's comprehension of this biblical theology and his attempt to contextualize it must not be confused with the authenticity of the biblical theology itself. The Bible is not a consensus of theologies but an integrated Word of God. Belief in the unique inspiration of the Scriptures by the Holy Spirit is followed by confidence in the Holy Spirit to rightly illuminate the mind of the humble believer.

The Reformation principle of perspicuity is a valid corollary of this belief. Luther linked it with the priesthood of all believers. The Bible is understandable on its own terms and is its own most faithful interpreter. The Bible is to be interpreted in the literal or intended sense of the writers, as prose, poetry, typology, apocalyptic and so forth. The Reformers sought to correct the excessive allegorizing of Origen and the medieval church by this principle. Evangelicals recognize that the Bible is culturally conditioned and that in the providence of God this is also under the control of his unique revelation. However, this fact does not annul the Bible's essential perspicuity. For example, despite our lack of knowledge of the author and the particular context of its writing, the message of the Epistle to the Hebrews is clear in its essentials to all who acknowledge Christ's lordship and who "know the Scriptures and the power of God."

The Overruling Providence of God in
the Bible's Cultural Conditioning

Evangelicals recognize the inseparable connection between biblical event and interpretation. In conceptual terms there is an inseparable relationship between the content and form of the Word of God. Both are overshadowed by the Holy Spirit so that the inscripturated Word is the authoritative Word that God intended. This biblical content-form carries its own objectivity. It is not dependent on the relativity of the interpreter's own culture or the culture into which he contextualizes it.

God in his sovereignty chose a Semitic Hebrew culture through which to reveal his Word. If he had chosen a Chinese or an Indian cultural form, the content of the Word would have been different, for to radically change the form which carries its own world view and set of values is to change the content. In the same way God incarnate took the form of a son and not of a daughter. Those living in a religious culture in which amoral goddesses are worshiped and in which mystical cultic practices are associated with the worship of the Divine Mother will understand why God did not reveal himself as a daughter.

In divine wisdom God chose Abram out of a Mesopotamian culture and through his descendants formed a carrier culture that reflected the interaction of the supra-cultural content and the cultural form. Thus there is a uniqueness about the Hebrew culture of the Bible, both Old and New Testament. It is not just a culture alongside any other culture, but it became a unique culture that carried the marks of the divine-human interaction. In the providence of God this culture was able to faithfully carry the uniqueness of the divine message of creation, sin, redemption and supremely the Incarnation and resurrection of the divine Son.

Jesus Christ was born a Jew, and it is an affront to divine sovereignty to speak of a black Christ or an Indian or Italian Christ. If the Hindu, Buddhist or pagan European tribal culture of two thousand years ago, each with its own world view, moral values and institutions, had been the carrier of the gospel, then the content of the gospel would have been radically changed. Mbiti and other African scholars have noted the affinity between many African concepts and practices and the Old Testament, but even here it must be seriously questioned that the world view of African traditional religion could have been an adequate form for the biblical content.

The Old Testament reflects the profound interaction of the supra-cultural revealed Word and the cultural life of the Hebrews and those of the surrounding nations. In the formation of a covenanted people as "my people" God transformed some of these cultural forms such as circumcision to his purposes and rejected others such as idolatry. God called Abraham and his family into a covenant relationship of faith and obedience. The story of the patriarchs is a story of the progressive de-culturalization of elements conflicting with divine self-disclosure, such as Canaanite concepts of El, the Baals and probably the personal name of Yahweh as the Lord God. During the pilgrimage of the Israelites as nomads in the Promised Land, followed by their captivity in Egypt and then during the wilderness journey, undesirable elements of the surrounding culture were progressively weakened and eliminated. Idolatry, pagan sexual morality, corrupt economic and political practices came under the judgment of God.

Moreover, the prophets of the Lord from Moses to John the Baptist rebuked false attempts at contextualization and pointed forward to the coming of the kingdom of God on earth and his lordship over a new covenant people of God. The story of the judges, the institutionalized kingdom, the exile and the restored remnant all point to the divine sovereignty preserving the Word of God against the corrupt conditioning of pagan culture.

All human cultures have a natural tendency to harmonize a trans-cultural message within their own cultic world view and practice. The Old Testament is very largely the record of the struggle against the syncretistic tendency of the Baalization of Yahweh worship which continued from the patriarchs until the exile. In times of self-confidence and independence when Israel was proud of her nationhood, victorious over her enemies and in possession of her land, her faith was noticeably and falsely conditioned by the surrounding cultures. In these times pagan religious ideas and cultural practices such as mixed marriages were encouraged. But then God raised up his judges and prophets such as Samuel, Elijah and Jeremiah, who called the people to repentance and purity of faith. God punished the Israelites by allowing their enemies to subjugate them. In their suffering they cried out for mercy and they learned once more to trust in the covenant promises of God and to obey his laws.

At times of faith and dependence on God, the people of God acknowledged his lordship over their total behavior and the degree of false cultural conditioning by the neighboring cultures became minimal and the rebuke of the prophets effective. This acknowledging of God's lordship over history by the covenant people transformed cultural conditioning from a problem and a curse to a channel of revelation and grace. The transformed function of circumcision is a case in point, but later degeneration turned it into a stumbling block to true faith.

In the New Testament era, the biblical writers, whose authority and message belonged to the apostolic tradition of the primitive church, wrote from within a Hebrew cultural framework. However, in the fulfillment of the Lord's commission to communicate the gospel to the whole world, which included the Hellenistic as well as the Judaistic cultures, the New Testament writers utilized contemporary forms of religious expression as modes of communication. They adopted and transformed some Hellenistic and pagan language forms and rejected others.

For example, a key word such as *eros* (sensual love) was rejected, while concepts such as *mythos* (myth) and *daimon* (demon) were only used in a negative sense. They utilized words that were common to both the Septuagint and to Hellenistic philosophy, such as *kyrios* (lord), *logos* (word) and *soter* (savior), but in ways that were consistent with the Hebrew usage.

Some words which were prominent in Hellenistic culture, such as *mysterion* (mystery), were transformed and used in a totally new setting. In the Hellenistic cults *mysterion* belonged to the cultic practice in which participants received a secret initiation in order to experience identification with the deity and his cosmic power. Paul used *mysterion* in the Jewish sense of a special revelation made by God about his plans for the future. God's power was revealed in the disclosure of the secret not in the keeping of it (Eph. 1:9; 3:3; 6:19; Col. 1:26-27).

Metamorphosis (transformation or transfiguration) is an example of one of the few cases where a Greek religious term, which appears to have no Old Testament or Jewish background, was given a new biblical meaning.[61] More attention needs to be given to applying these biblical models to the problem of cross-cultural communication in our own contexts.

Hermeneutical Principles for Understanding Biblical Theology
We must draw together some hermeneutical principles that have been inherent in the discussion so far. The interpreter's first task is to hear the Word of God as given through the plurality of the biblical writers and so comprehend it that he can faithfully interpret it to others. The evangelical interpreter looks to the Scriptures themselves to discern these hermeneutical principles in this process of cross-cultural communication. These principles will include:

1. *The lifestyle principle of faith-commitment.* Consequent upon conversion, a resting confidence in the heavenly Father, total submission to the lordship of Christ, and sensitivity and obedience to the Holy Spirit are the essential beginnings necessary for bib-

lical understanding. To those who were confused over the resurrection Jesus said, "You are wrong, because you know neither the scriptures nor the power of God" (Mt. 22:29). Without living the life of faith no one can understand the truth of the Word of God. The dictum of Anselm, *credo ut intelligam* (I believe so I may understand), is at the heart of the historic evangelical tradition. It is fundamental to comprehending true biblical theology and to faithful contextualization.

2. *The objective-subjective principle of distancing from and identification with the text.* A biblically determined hermeneutic involves a two-way process of encounter between the interpreter and the Word of God on one hand and the interpreter and the receptor's culture on the other. This two-way process seeks to maintain the balance between the objective authority of the Word of God and the subjective experience of the interpretation. The widely accepted principle of Bultmann's hermeneutical circle needs fresh interpretation by evangelicals.[62]

The objective-subjective principle involves the interpreter's encounter and response with both the Word of God and with his own culture and that of the receptor. It presumes a two-way process of distancing oneself from the text (involving critical study and reflection) and then fusion or identification with the text (involving commitment and obedience).[63] The task of exegesis is the recovery of the *sensus literalis*, the literal or natural meaning of the text, involving the right use of the linguistic tools and historical method, traditionally known as the "grammatico-historical" method. The purpose of this method is to discover what the biblical writer said, and it must be distinguished from the more speculative historical critical method which aims to discover the author's intention. In seeking to distance himself from the text, the interpreter will seek to critically let his own pre-understanding be corrected by the text itself, recognizing its objective authority and its internal harmony. To use Ernst Fuchs striking phrase, "The texts must translate us before we translate them."[64] Thus the interpreter will seek to relate one passage of Scripture to another and to interpret one passage by another.

The interpreter's response in the process is one of fusion or identification with the message of the text. This principle has always been well understood by evangelicals, especially those within the pietistic tradition. The interpreter receives the Word as God's word to his own heart. This principle reinforces the principle of perspicuity as the illuminating work of the Holy Spirit. It is illustrated by the prayer of the psalmist and a key text of the Scripture Union movement: "Thy word have I hid in mine heart, that I might not sin against thee" (Ps. 119:11 AV). This "fusion of horizons," to use Hans-Georg Gadamer's phrase, is fundamental to any exegetical method leading to an understanding of biblical and dogmatic theology.

The same two-way process is essential in the interpreter's encounter and response with the receptor of the Word and with his culture. This is the task of contextualizing theology, and it is set in the framework of the church's mission in the world. Its goal is cross-cultural communication for evangelism and service. Much of the misunderstanding of contextualization has arisen through a failure to distinguish the two-way process of contextualizing the Word in a specific cultural situation and the exegetical task of comprehending biblical or dogmatic theology as an authoritative base from which to contextualize theology.

For the interpreter to distance himself from the cultural situation (his own and the receptor's) is to exercise the prophetic ministry. We have already referred to the functioning of the prophetic principle in the cultural conditioning of the Bible itself; the same principle is valid in the process of contextualization. By the prophetic principle the interpreter critically judges his own culture and pre-understanding and also that of the cultural assumptions and behavior of those to whom the message is being proclaimed.

One example is sufficient. It has often been pointed out that the category of God as "father" is inadequate in a matrilineal society, as for example among certain tribes in Africa and in Asia, and that therefore alternative symbols for God should be considered.[65] Instead of semi-absolutizing the local cultural institution of the family and accommodating the Word of God to it, the prophetic principle will allow the biblical revelation to judge the interpreter's image of "father." This means that the concept of God as father will need careful explanation in translating and interpreting it in a matrilineal society. To accommodate a pagan image apart from the transforming power of the prophetic principle only opens the door to syncretism.

But distancing must be followed by identification with the receptor's culture. For example, the tenderness and patience of God would be readily understood in a matrilineal society. The Incarnation is the absolute model of this identification involving both renunciation and identification. There will be no real cross-cultural communication apart from this identification. It begins as an attitude of mind (Phil. 2:5) and leads on to the practice of costly servanthood (Phil. 2:5-8). This is the missionary calling of the church, the price to be paid for true contextualization.

3. *The bodylife principle of the believing community.* The hermeneutical task is not a private or purely individual one; it is the responsibility of the whole body of Christ and must be undertaken within the framework of the believing community. Together, the people of God are a royal priesthood, a household of faith built upon the foundation of the apostles and the prophets, Jesus Christ being the chief cornerstone (Eph. 2:20). The Holy Spirit illuminates the individual interpreter within the context of the church. True contextualization of the gospel takes place in the church and not in the world. It is not man's work but God's.

Two aspects of this bodylife principle are important to the hermeneutic task: first, the recognition that the Spirit gives gifts to members of the body. Not all are apostles, prophets, teachers, pastors, helpers, but all are dependent on each other for the building up of the body of Christ. Therefore, the biblical scholar with his expertise in the grammatico-historical method of exegesis needs the help of the evangelist with his gift of preaching. The pastor with his knowledge of anthropological and sociological principles complements the ministry of the prophet. Hermeneutics can only be done in the context of the whole body.

Second, the body has an historical dimension. The contemporary interpretive process is in fact the continuation of the interpretive process throughout the history of the church. Contextualization did not begin with the coining of the word. Therefore, the true interpreter will seek to understand the commentaries and theological writings of the church Fathers, the Reformers and theologians of other cultures. An evangelical will discern insights into the Word of God in the writings of Catholic and the Orthodox scholars. The creeds and confessions of the church will be utilized in the interpretive process. A thorough knowledge of church history will provide a balance to any overreaction against Western forms of contextualized theology. Many of the issues of contextualization in the Third World today are in essence similar to those faced by the early church Fathers and by the later European Reformers.

4. *The mission-in-the-world principle.* The framework for the hermeneutical task is the mission of God in the world. Hermeneutics begins with the recognition of the distinction between the two supra-cultural kingdoms—the kingdom of God and the kingdom of Satan—and the distinction between the church and the world. The impact of secularism on theology has been to blur the distinction between the church and the world so that the world rather than the church is the center of God's activity. The culmination of this secularizing process is the salvation of all history as expounded in contemporary liberation theologies. But only when the biblical distinctives are maintained will the process of contextualizing the gospel in a particular situation conform to the norm of biblical theology. The church's mission in the world is broadly speaking worship and fellowship, social service and justice, and evangelizing and making disciples. Contextualized theology which does not serve this mission is a truncated theology.

4

The Dynamics of Cross-cultural Communication

The contextualizing of the gospel is the task of cross-cultural communication. It has three centers or foci: the encultured gospel of the Bible, the messenger or communicator who belongs to another culture and the receiver of the gospel who responds from within the context of his own culture. Even if the communicator inherits the same cultural framework as the receiver, he is always a distinct focal center for he not only forms his pre-understanding from his and other cultures, but he has his own unique supra-cultural experience with the living God. The dynamics of cross-cultural communication are always missiological and are therefore always three-dimensional.

From Biblical to Contextualized Theology
Contextualized theology as distinct from dogmatic biblical theology is always relative. The communicator has a fallible knowledge of the gospel. Any particular contextual formulation of theology may be valid and true to the gospel, but it cannot claim to comprehend the totality of the revealed Word of God. All contextualized formulations remain inadequate. There is therefore a relativity in

comprehension of the whole message of God. The hermeneutical process of distancing and of identification, exercised under the lordship of Christ and the Holy Spirit, ought to ensure a progressive approximation of the communicator's understanding of the gospel to its biblical formulation.

Human culture is always a dynamic process for the design for living. It gathers up the traditions of the past, responds and accommodates to the modernity of a technological and increasingly urban society and is in constant interaction with the supra-cultural principalities and powers. As we have seen each generation learns afresh and formulates its own culture. There is therefore a great degree of flexibility and relativity in the focal center of human culture.

The contextualization of relational centers. The history of the church is a history of contextualized theologies that are varying responses to the work of the Spirit of God in particular historical contexts. The truer they are to the givenness of biblical theology the more complementary and the less contradictory they become. For example, Luther's understanding of justification by faith as the relational center for his theologizing was the necessary biblical answer to the confused thinking of a corrupt medieval church. Although Lutheranism is a Western contextualized theology, its formulation of justification by faith is extremely relevant throughout the Third World. In the context of the Hindu notion of *karma* and the total lack of assurance of salvation, I believe the recovery of justification by faith is one of the greatest needs in the formulation of an Indian Christian theology. However, a commentary on Galatians by an Indian Christian theologian will be contextualized in a very different way from that of Luther's commentary.

The traditions of Reformed theology with its relational center in the covenant has particular relevance for the church in Islamic cultures. It is significant that the majority of churches and missions witnessing in Islamic societies are Presbyterian or Anglican in the Reformed tradition. John Wesley's overwhelming experience of the love of God and of his grace in Christ spoke not only to the deepest needs of the lower and oppressed classes of English society in the context of a national church that was rationalistic and deistic, but it has had an amazing appeal to ordinary people world-wide. The modern pentecostal movement with its discovery of the power of the Holy Spirit has liberated Christians enslaved in legalistic religion and brought spiritual life to the poor and oppressed especially in Latin America. In the present reaction to the Western imperialistic theologies, these biblically framed relational centers must not be lost.

There are, however, other truths of the gospel which may give birth to new movements. Hopefully some will begin in non-Western churches. Hindu and Buddhist Asia is ripe for a fresh contextualization of the doctrine of creation and resurrection, Latin America for a theology of the kingdom of God. Africa and the Pacific have yet to contextualize their joyous experience of the lordship of Christ. Those suffering under Marxist or military dictatorships make Christ the liberator, the center of their theologizing. But if these contextualized theologies are to quench the spiritual thirst of people of the world, they must be constantly subjected to the norms of biblical theology.

Starting from within the circle of faith-commitment. Cross-cultural communication of the gospel does not go unchallenged. Since World War 2 the relevance of the gospel for the modern world has been challenged at many points. The rapid acceleration of the process of secularization has made the claims of the gospel seem irrelevant for many who are poor and oppressed. The atheism of materially determined Marxism has denied the existence of God. The behavioral psychology of B. F. Skinner and others proclaimed man the master of his fate. The resurgence, and in some cases the recovery, of the missionary zeal of world faiths have forced many Christians to accept a *status quo* and turn from evangelism to dialogue in the search for harmony in the world community.

The contextualizing of biblical theology in a changing world demands a rethinking of the whole process of doing theology. But the Bible itself insists that the starting point must be from within the circle of faith-commitment to God's self-revelation in Christ. With the weakening of assurance of the knowledge of the content of the Christian faith, many theologians and communicators are, in practice, making the cultural context the starting point. This is the way of "natural theology" and leads to a cul-de-sac. But, as the history of natural theology from Thomas Aquinas to the present has shown, it is not possible to jump from the God of the philosophers to the God of Abraham, Isaac and Jacob, who is the Father of our Lord Jesus Christ. "Of Him," says Klaas Runia, "one can speak only from within the circle of faith."[66] There is no way to move from nature to grace. Karl Barth's constant attack on natural theology is well founded. The mystery of faith begins with the knowledge of Christ and not with philosophy and human tradition (Col. 2:1-8).

The biblical writers, early apologists and Christian evangelists have, however, always looked for some common ground on which to defend the faith and to proclaim the gospel. Paul's Areopagus address (Acts 17:19-34) is the classical model. Philosophy is a bridgehead to proclaim the gospel. Narayan Vaman Tilak, the Charles Wesley of India, claimed he came to Christ "over the bridge of Tukaram" (the seventeenth-century Hindu bhakti poet of western India). Evidences and rational argument prepare for and confirm faith but do not prove the argument of faith. True dialogue between Christians and those of other faiths and ideologies begins with the premise of the Christian confessing his faith in Christ.

If the starting point is the circle of faith-commitment, then the content of faith is the uniqueness of the acts of the Trinitarian God.[67] The doctrine of the Triune God in Scripture is not a rationally formulated doctrine. The dogma came centuries later with Athanasius and Augustine in the context of the Christological controversy over the deity of Christ and the nature of his person, and at a later stage a similar debate took place over the Holy Spirit. While we believe the formulations of Chalcedon are faithful to the biblical teaching of the Triune God, the language used may not be the most appropriate in a different cultural context. The Trinitarian nature of God was the functional theology of those uniquely inspired responding to the progressive self-disclosure of God himself. The Trinity is a divine mystery because it is supracultural. The unity of God manifest "in three different personal ways" is beyond the speculative or rational comprehension of any religious or philosophical system.[68]

Throughout the history of the church there have been many attempts to make the doctrine of the Trinity more acceptable by using analogies and illustrations drawn largely from creation itself. Some have likened it to the three modes of water as steam, water and ice, others to the sun as the orb, its light and power, yet others to the mathematical symbols of one to the power of three equals one. Augustine used the analogy of the root, trunk and branch of a tree. George David has used the psychological terminology of "a shared relational self."[69]

These analogies may confirm faith, but they do not create it. They generally carry the danger of modalism, of God appearing in three forms as with the Hindu *trimurti*. The Christian use of the term *person* is less than satisfactory as the term carries the overtones of individualism leading to a false tritheism. Yet Runia concludes, "God not only reveals Himself as Father, Son and Holy Spirit but God is Father, Son and Holy Spirit."[70] This is the mystery of our faith that revealed doctrines precede our experiencing of them but that the systematic and contextualizing of them follows our experience of God from within the circle of faith-commitment.

The Gospel Is the Revelation of God as Creator-Savior
Much theological confusion has been created by isolating God the Savior from God the Creator and also by blurring the distinction between his work of creation and of redemption. Any true contextualization of the gospel must reflect the biblical norm of the inseparable but distinct work of the Creator-Savior.

The foundation statement of creation (Gen. 1—2) is not an isolated objective formula but is the confession of the covenanted people of Israel who had experienced God's saving grace, mediated through Moses and the Law, and to whom was revealed the doctrine of creation. The placing of the creation narrative within the Pentateuch puts God's original act in the context of his saving acts. In comparison, the Hindu vedic account of creation, as with the Babylonian accounts, sets creation in a mythological framework in which the gods and creation belong to a closed system.

In the New Testament, God's work as Creator is always in the context of his work as Savior. God's work in creation and Incarnation culminates in the resurrection of Christ. In the discovery of the bodily resurrection of Jesus Christ, Thomas cries out, "My Lord and my God!" (Jn. 20:28). The great Christological passages of Paul, especially Ephesians 1, Philippians 2:5-11 and Colossians 1:15-20 hold together God in Christ as Creator and Savior. In Romans 8 the redemption of the whole of creation is in the context of the children of God who cry "Abba Father." God's work as Savior beginning with the Fall leads to the once-and-for-all atonement in the cross and culminates in the return of the King and the establishment of the kingdom of God on earth. These two lines of God's activity, creation and redemption meet in the Incarnation, the death and resurrection of Jesus Christ, the Son of God.

In the interpreting of this message to people of another culture, the lordship of Christ as Creator-Savior is the unchanging universal and the norm by which all cultural understandings of creation and redemption must be judged and either rejected or transformed.

The revelation of the Triune God is always as the living God. He is eternal life. The central mark distinguishing human beings from the animal kingdom is that God created humans with the capacity to experience this life. In creation it was by a supernatural act that people were created in the image of God. In redemption it is by a supernatural act of God the Holy Spirit that they are born again and receive eternal life. God is a spirit who transcends creation and yet he is immanent in it. The living God is a holy God and his Spirit a Holy Spirit. Because the living God is Triune, he is the eternal communicator and the nature of his communication is love. God is love. The Father always loves the Son and the Son always loves the Father, and the Holy Spirit is the agent of this relationship of love. The living God is sovereign over creation and redemption. He predestines, he foreknows, he is absolute freedom. The world is derived and dependent on him; he is not dependent on it. Both creation and redemption are the work of God's love.

A full-orbed doctrine of the Creator-Savior is fundamental to any faithful contextualizing of theology and is the basis for evaluating all other religious understandings of creation and redemption. False contextualization begins with an inadequate understanding of the Triune God as Creator-Savior. The natural religions are always reductionist. They reduce the living personal God to an impersonal principle or absolute. They reduce love and holiness to fate and capriciousness. They reduce the freedom of love to the bondage of law. All natural religions and philosophies—whether the neo-platonism, idealism, logical positivism and existentialism of the West, or the *advaita vedanta* of India, or the moralism of Confucianism, the impermanence of reality of Buddhism or the spirit world of African traditional religions—fall short of the biblical Triune God. Allah of Islam is also a rational reduction of the Triune God.

Against this background of normative natural religion, the three-relational-centered God stands in contrast to all forms of Eastern or Western claims to pantheism. In the faith of the covenanted people of Israel and of the church there is a true mysticism of being "in Christ" and of belonging to one body, but there is never a loss of personal distinction as in pantheism. The gap between creation and redemption is never closed. In the Triune Creator-Savior God there is no room for religious deism as in Judaism and Islam, where predestination is reduced to fatalism, love to submission to law and the sovereign God to a God who could not suffer.

Again, there is no room for the pan-en-theism of the humanist process theology which seeks to bridge or fuse together the Personal and the All, the Creator and the Redeemer, heaven and hell. Pan-en-theism is the ground of much contemporary universalism, the hope of dialogical theology. It is the normative path to a synthesis of truth and error on the plane of relativity. In both the West and the Third World current pan-en-theistic theologies are perhaps the greatest threat to evangelism and to the growth of the church.

Further, the distinguishing mark of the image of God in human beings is the special relationship between God and people symbolized in the relationship of a father to a child, by which a child may call God his Father.[71] It points forward to the new creation of adoption into the family of God (Rom. 8:15; Gal. 4:5). Christ is the first fruits of this new creation who in his ascension manifests the same unique relationship to the Father that he manifested in his incarnate life. The church, as the household of faith reflecting the newness of this relationship, ought to be the place where the contextualization of this image of father-child is most clearly manifest in a world of broken human relationships. The church must become the extended family of God.

From Alienation and Idolatry to Death and Re-Creation

The human problem is a problem of alienation. It is a dual problem of alienation from God and from one's neighbor. The primary difficulty in the communication of the gospel is that mankind, as individuals and as corporate units of society, do not recognize the true nature of this alienation. Some may be obsessed with the problem of their *avidya* or ignorance of their true union with God so that they, like the sadhu, are oblivious to the social and economic needs of their neighbors and to the injustices of society. Others, however, may be so obsessed with the problems of poverty, unemployment, social injustice and political corruption that they are no longer aware of the dimension of their alienation from God. This double blindness is found in every religious and secular culture.

The biblical doctrine of alienation begins in Genesis 3 where man and woman suppress the knowledge of God, rebel against his lordship and seek to make themselves equal to God. Paul gives a carefully worded theological interpretation of this alienation (Rom. 1:18-32). Sin in its ultimate form is described as idolatry, in which the creature creates deity in his own image or that of the created world and through magical identification placates or controls his gods, only to become a slave of his own creation. The end is subjection to demonic powers, spiritual and eternal death. Western contextualized theologies have not always realized the importance of sin as idolatry, although they have some knowledge of the occult, which is one form of the demonic power of mystical identification. In religions that recognize a supreme God, idolatry may take the form of the manipulation of the sacred words of Scripture or of submission to law in order to control God. Whether by a process of mysticism or by rationalism, in every case man is his own savior from alienation. The alienation described in Genesis 3 inevitably leads to the form of alienation described in Genesis 4, people oppressing each other, ending in violence and death. Because the Fall affected every person and all of creation, the social, economic and political forms of alienation which begin in Genesis 4 reach to the final fragmentation of language and community described in Genesis 11.

The prophet is God's agent to pronounce judgment on all forms of alienation. The prophets of Israel and Judah rebuked both religious idolatry and social injustice. Amos, for example, rebuked Israel's syncretistic worship (2:4; 4:4-5; 5:21) and the rich, including their wives, for their disproportionate wealth (3:15; 4:1; 6:4) and for their oppression of the poor (2:6; 6:1-7). Thus, true contextualization of the gospel calls for both spiritual renewal and for social justice.

The gospel brings a new and deeper dimension of alienation to those cultures which interpret alienation solely in terms of social shame, as in Buddhist society. To legalistic societies, such as Islam, which know little of love and forgiveness, to societies which fear the spirit world and to those which fear the secret police of secular governments, the gospel offers a new perspective on alienation. Twentieth-century forms of alienation are only new forms of those of the nineteenth century. *The Willowbank Report* suggests that cannibalism now takes the form of social injustice which eats the poor widow; strangling is the oppression of the poor; infanticide is abortion; patricide is the criminal neglect of senior citizens; ritual prostitution is sexual promiscuity, and tribal wars are World Wars 1 and 2.[72]

The prophetic ministry of the gospel calls for a de-culturalization in every culture of the accretions to true faith. From Moses to John the Baptist, the biblical prophets condemned elements of culture which were contrary to the Word of God. At the same time the prophet's ministry fulfills and re-creates the truths of every culture. The gospel renews and transforms those elements of culture which are true to God's general revelation. As the Lausanne Covenant stated, "Because man is God's creature, some of his culture is rich in beauty and goodness" (para. 10). At the deepest cultural level of world view the gospel takes the African awareness of spirit reality and brings new dimensions into the African peoples' understanding of their secular work and of their worship as involving the whole of life.

As we have noted, however, the starting point is not culture but the Word of God. Many contemporary Third World theologies, like some Western theologies, are seeking for areas of fulfillment in the gospel and the life of the church of the beliefs and practices of other religious faiths. This is the way of natural theology and inevitably leads to syncretism.

The evangelical, however, begins the process of contextualization with the unique and final revelation of God in Christ and the gospel which he interprets in the context of his own and the receiver's culture. To do this in a relevant way he must understand the cultural context and the questions which it raises. He must study both the Bible and the newspaper. But the process of theologizing is a one-way street. The gospel judges all of culture and not just some of it, destroying what is contrary to the Word of God and re-creating what is true to God's universal revelation to mankind. This is the way of the Spirit-controlled prophet and pastor. We may illustrate this process in the areas of worship and the family in Indian culture.

Worship is the deepest expression of a religious world view, and both beauty and ugliness are invariably associated with it as in religious art, music and poetry. It is in worship that true contextualization ought to be most clearly seen, expressing the true adoration of God. At the level of moral values, contextualization of the gospel will lead to judgment and renewal of conscience as man's sensitive response to the Word of the living God and the dictates of his moral law.

For example, the Hindu concept of *karma*, in its essence, glimpses the truth of the biblical injunction, "as a man sows so shall he reap." But it must be cleansed of its philosophic and pagan religious accretions if it is to be used in interpreting the law of God as described in the Old Testament and in the ethical manifesto of the Sermon on the Mount. In Hindu culture, *karma* is usually divorced from the lawgiver and becomes an absolute principle to which even the gods are subject. It is the abuse of biblical law, making law into a way of salvation (as in Judaism). It becomes a tyrannical master so that forgiveness is impossible and any idea of substitutionary atonement is absurd. It ends in a line of despair, meaninglessness and silence. Therefore, the contextualization of biblical law will destroy all that is false and evil in *karma* and will re-create all that is true according to the Word of God. *Karma* then becomes a meeting point and religious and cultural bridge for communicating the gospel to Hindus.

The family is one institution of any culture that is critical for the contextualization process. God created man, male and female, with the family as the basic relational unit of society (Gen. 2:18-24). Marriage and the family belong to the creation order and may be enjoyed by peoples of all cultures who live according to the creation principle of Genesis 2:24. Mbiti speaks with warm appreciation of the African home as the center of nurture and education with its strong sense of mutual interdependence and sustaining force in times of need.[73] This is equally true of many Asian cultures. In New Delhi many Hindu, Muslim and Sikh neighbors live satisfying family lives. But alas, when people pervert the biblical understanding of the family with the father as head, abuse sex outside of marriage, enter into divorce and remarriage, practice homosexuality and abandon the elderly, then marriage and the family come under the judgment of God. The contextualization of the gospel in Hindu culture will not destroy the fabric of the Hindu joint family, but it will condemn elements that are contrary to the biblical model. For example, when a young man marries,his prime relationship will cease to be with his mother and will instead be transferred to his wife, contrary to Hindu tradition. At the same time it will transform the biblically true concepts of the Indian joint family such as respect for parents and sharing according to need. This model stands in judgment over the individualism and marital breakdown of many Western nuclear families. The biblical view will bring with it new elements of forgiveness and grace in marriage and a new understanding of the basis for arranging marriages and the giving of dowry that will enrich marriage so that it becomes a truly Indian Christian marriage and home.

The Universals and Variables in the Indigenous Church

The crisis in many churches today is one of self-identity. This is especially true of churches which are small and socially weak minority communities struggling for existence in hostile situations. They tend to overreact either in identification with their national culture or in the rejection of it, usually in favor of a Western culture inherited from the missionary movement. As the Lausanne Covenant stated, "The church must be in the world; the world must not be in the Church" (para. 12).

There is always a dynamic tension between the supra-cultural universals of the church common to churches worldwide, and the cultural variables peculiar to each national church. In relation to the supra-cultural nature of the church as the body of Christ there must be a "formal correspondence" among all churches to the divinely appointed concept of the church as given in the Scriptures. In relation to the particular cultures in which the church is contextualized we expect the gospel to make a dynamic impact on their design for living equivalent to the impact that the biblical people of God made on their own societies. Unless this creative tension is maintained between the "formal correspondence" of the universals and the "dynamic equivalence" of cultural variables, there will be no true contextualization of the church.

The universals of the church are the universals of the kingdom of God expressed in terms of a new humanity, a new society and a new eschatological hope. The new humanity is the new man in Christ being conformed to the image of Christ, the glory of God (2 Cor. 4:4). This new humanity is made visible through the fruits of the Spirit as virtues that have universal expression (Gal. 5:22). Insofar as Christ is Lord of his people the church is the visible agent of the kingdom. The signs of the kingdom include the evidence of Christ's power to heal the blind, the lame and the leper, and to raise the dead (Mt. 11:2-5), and to demonstrate Christ's power over principalities and powers.

The church universal has a common hope of the consummation of the kingdom at the final Day of the Lord, when the whole of creation now in bondage, will be liberated (Rom. 8:19-23). The church universal shares a common faith-commitment to Christ, a common focus of worship, a *koinonia* or fellowship that transcends all barriers of race, social status and sex. It is a pilgrim church which since Abraham has looked forward to the city which has foundations, whose builder and maker is God (Heb. 11:10). The universality of the church is manifested in moral absolutes derived from the moral laws of the Old Testament and the Sermon on the Mount in the New; these absolutes stand in judgment against the ethical standards of all cultures.

In the birth and growth of local churches there ought to be a progression in conformity to the pattern of behavior as it progressively developed through biblical history. Some categories of moral behavior, such as social discriminations, slavery and polygamy may slowly disappear only as the church grows in subjection to Christ and his kingdom, as it did in biblical history.

The pattern of New Testament church life and witness was simple and flexible. Structures and patterns of church behavior developed according to the needs of the new community. The New Testament gives us a ground plan rather than a blueprint for church life. The same ought to be true today. The structures and government of the church, the forms of her worship, sacraments and communal fellowship, the methods of communicating the gospel and patterns for service in the world, ought to reflect the cultural variables and meet the particular needs of each community.

Mbiti rightly appeals for a sensitive and sympathetic use of African cultural forms in the worship, the community life, church nurture and education, Christian values and ethics, and Christian service and witness.[74] He points to the many elements of African life and worship which had much in common with biblical Semitic culture, but he recognizes that many other elements come under the judgment of the gospel. He concludes, "I believe that Africa is spiritually capable of bringing its contribution of glory to the city of God, through the elements of our religiosity and culture— healed, saved, purified and sanctified by the Gospel." [75]

This helpful statement, however, carries the seeds of natural theology. It would be better to reverse the order and say that the glory of the city of God is seen in the healing, saving, purifying and sanctifying of elements of African spirituality. The difference

may appear small, but the consequences for theological understanding are great. It is a difference of methodology and the way we
do theology.

Without the formal correspondence principles of Scripture it is
not possible to make right value judgments on these variable cultural factors. The dynamic equivalence principle is necessarily
subjective. Throughout the history of the church accommodation
to cultural accretions and provincialism have destroyed the life of
many churches. The local or national church must never become
captive to its own culture.

The teaching ministry of the church is a crucial area in the effec-
tiveness or failure of the contextualizing of the church. The cur-
riculum of our theological institutions, concepts of theological imperialism or of theological excellence and methods of examination
easily become tools of provincialism. The transference of models
of theological training from one culture to another can become a
serious hindrance to the effective proclamation of the gospel and
the building of churches that are both biblically faithful and culturally relevant. Evangelical theological educators in Africa, Asia
and Latin America are recognizing the need for evangelical associations of schools and of theologians in order to grapple effectively
with these issues.

The Cross-cultural Communication of the Gospel
The dynamic tension between universality and convertibility in
the indigenization of the church also applies to the communication
of the gospel. Contextualization can only take place in the context
of mission. Andrew Kirk rightly says, "Our belief is that the only
proper context for serious theological thought is the growth of the
Church in its triple mission of worship, prophetic and diaconic
engagement in the world, and evangelism."[76] Contextualization is
a missiological task. The one supreme missiological model is the
Incarnation. Our mission is modeled on his: "As the Father has
sent me, even so I send you" (Jn. 20:21).

The *Willowbank Report* drew attention to the double action in
the mind of Christ leading him to a renunciation of state, independence and immunity, and an identification (without loss of his own

identity) with us, and especially with the poor and the powerless.[77] Cross-cultural communication is a call to be a humble messenger of the gospel. Because the gospel is nonnegotiable the messenger of the gospel must adopt the servant role of the Master if the arrogance of theological and cultural superiority is to be avoided. "A Church which preaches the Cross must itself be marked by the Cross" (para. 6).

The Holy Spirit is always the cross-cultural missionary. He goes before to prepare the way for the gospel, he uses human wrath to praise him, he makes Nebuchadnezzar and Cyrus the servants of the Lord. He convicts of sin and of judgment, even those who have never heard of the name of Christ. In God's general revelation to mankind he speaks to all people through the witness of nature and the inner promptings of conscience, so that all are without excuse.

Saving revelation and saving grace are always supernatural and supra-cultural. Effective cross-cultural communication requires a clear theological distinction between God's general revelation and his special revelation, though in the process of conversion and re-creation they can never be separated. Revelation is unitary. The former without the latter is powerless, and the latter without the former lacks the basis of the knowledge of God as Creator.

The only ground for the salvation of mankind throughout human history is the finality and efficacy of the cross, whether or not those who repent and believe understand its full implication. It is on this basis alone that the Holy Spirit may be pleased to call to salvation some who have never heard the name of Christ. On this agonizing issue Scripture is largely silent and we must resist the temptation to speculate. Our task is faithfully to communicate the gospel, using the bridges that the Holy Spirit has prepared in many and various ways.

Through a knowledge of the religious scriptures and customs of other cultures the faithful communicator of the gospel will perceive elements of God's general revelation and be able to effectively use them as bridges in communicating a knowledge of sin and a call to believe. In some cultures the concept of "blood sacrifice" can be used as a bridge, in others a "peace child." Islam with its special relationship to the Old Testament and to the gospel has many elements which carry a degree of what Kenneth Cragg has called "convertibility." Recognition of the divine unity, the obligation to render to God right worship, the total rejection of idolatry as expressed in Islamic worship, prayer, fasting, architecture and calligraphy, are elements that can be transformed and utilized in cross-cultural evangelism.

True conversion involves a radical transformation of the whole of culture—world view, values, institutions and customs. The gospel rejects those elements which are contrary to the revelation of God, converts those that reflect man made in the image of God and creates new elements which are distinctive to the gospel.

Convertibility is not limited to traditional cultures but extends to the truths of secular and technological culture. M. M. Thomas has drawn attention to the liberating elements from superstition in modern secular culture and their place in humanization as salvation offered by Christ, the true man.[78]

True contextualization in mission concerns the needs of people in society as well as in their relation to God. It concerns people oppressing others as well as human suppression of God. It involves the social, economic and political macrostructures of society and the impact on them of modern technology and ideological propaganda. Contextualization is concerned with the principalities and powers in spiritual places and with the institutionalized power structures of capitalistic and socialistic political systems. Therefore, evangelism as reconciling people to God must not be isolated from social service and justice by which people are reconciled with each other. Contextualization involves the ministry of both the prophet and the evangelist.

Evangelical prophets have usually been strong in rebuking individual and personal sins against God and one's neighbor, but often weak in discerning the nature of social sins such as tribalism and racism, economic monopolies and political blackmail, the misuse of environmental resources and wars of greed. Such sins are often covered up by acceptable social structures, and we have few prophets who speak against them. The Willowbank Report states, "Perhaps the most insidious form of syncretism in the world today is the attempt to mix a privatized gospel of personal forgiveness with a worldly (even demonic) attitude to wealth and power."[79]

True and faithful communication of the gospel begins with the contextualization of the gospel in the life of the communicator. This takes place through worship and fellowship, through diaconic service and prophetic justice and through evangelistic witness and disciplemaking. Contextualization demands the willing acceptance of the lordship of Christ and joyous servanthood and suffering for others. The church as the people of God is called to take the whole gospel to the whole world, translating it into relevant cultural forms in order to produce the same fruit of love and righteousness that characterized the individuals, families and communities that comprised the early church. The gospel will remain unchanged but the church, in the analogy of rice planting, will share the continuity of the universal body of Christ and the particularity of historic but changing national cultures. The church in the world is called to be a model of the coming kingdom and the preserving salt and piercing light in a world that is corrupt and has lost its way.

A dynamic theology of gospel and culture is the necessary foundation for the fulfillment of the Great Commission and the work of the Holy Spirit recreating man in society after the image of Christ, the Creator-Savior. To God be the glory.

Notes

[1]Mahatma Gandhi, *Young India*, 22 Dec. 1917, cited in *Truth Is God* (M. K. Gandhi: Ahmedabad Navajivan Publishing House, 1955), p. 70.

[2]This problem was discussed in some depth at the Lausanne Congress in the Study Group "The Gospel, Contextualization and Syncretism." See report in *Let the Earth Hear His Voice*, ed. J. D. Douglas (Minneapolis: Worldwide Publications, 1975), pp. 1224-28.

[3]Sponsored by the Lausanne Theology and Education Group at Willowbank, Bermuda, January 6-13, 1978.

[4]*The Willowbank Report*: Lausanne Occasional Papers, No. 2 (Wheaton: Lausanne Committee for World Evangelization, 1978), p. 13.

[5]Ibid.

[6]Louis J. Luzbetak, *The Church and Cultures* (South Pasadena: William Carey Library, 1970), p. 61.

[7]John S. Mbiti, "Christianity and African Culture," *Journal of Theology of South Africa* (September 1977), p. 26.

[8]G. Linwood Barney, A revised unpublished edition of "The Supra Culture and the Cultural: Implications for Frontier Missions" in *The Gospel and Frontier Peoples*, ed. R. Pierce Beaver (South Pasadena: William Carey Library, 1973).

[9]Sir Norman Anderson, ed., *The World's Religions*, 4th ed., (London: InterVarsity Press, 1975), pp. 11-48.

[10]Mbiti, p. 27.

[11]Ibid., p. 29.

[12]TEF Staff, *Ministry in Context* (London: Theological Education Fund, 1972), p. 20.

[13]Ibid., p. 13.

[14]James O. Buswell, "Contextualization: Theory, Tradition and Method" in *Theology and Mission*, ed. David J. Hesselgrave (Grand Rapids: Baker Book House, 1978), pp. 93-94.

[15]*The Other Side* (March 1978), p. 62.

[16]David M. Paton, ed., *Breaking Barriers, Nairobi 1975* (London: SPCK; and Grand Rapids: Eerdmans, 1976), p. 254.

[17]See Charles H. Kraft, "The Contextualization of Theology," *Evangelical Missions Quarterly*, 14 (1978), 31-36.

[18]This issue surfaced at the Bermuda consultation. For a defense of the plurality of biblical theologies see *Partnership*, 15 Feb. 1978, No. 10.

[19]Daniel von Allmen, "The Birth of Theology," *International Review of Missions*, 44 (1975), 37-52.

[20]*WEF Theological News*, monograph No. 6 (April 1973).

[21]Von Allmen, pp. 41-42.

[22]Charles R. Taber argues that theology follows faith. He writes, "The apostles had a personal encounter with God in the Person of Jesus Christ, which they reflected upon and interpreted against the background of their own experience." "Is There More Than One Way to Do It Theology?" *Gospel and Context*, 1 (1978), 5. On the other hand, Ralph Martin argues that only on the ground of the early church's possessing a clearly defined body of revealed truth can we explain the Christian consciousness of the church's distinctive entity and its worship. *Worship in the Early Church* (London: Marshall, Morgan and Scott, 1974), p. 54ff.

[23]Von Allmen, p. 50.

[24]Ibid., p. 51.

[25]S. Wesley Ariarajah, "Towards a Theology of Dialogue," The Ecumenical Review, 29 (1977), 3-11.

[26]Ibid., p. 4.

[27]Ariarajah, p. 5.

[28]Ibid.

[29]Ibid., p. 8.

[30]Ibid., p. 9.

[31]Ibid., p. 4.

[32]Ibid., p. 11.

[33]Choan-seng Song, Christian Mission in Reconstruction: An Asian Attempt (Madras: CLS, 1975), p. 177.

[34]E. P. Nacpil, "The Critical Asian Principle," What Asian Christians Are Thinking, ed. D. J. Elwood (Quezon City, Philippines: New Day, 1976), pp. 3-6.

[35]The Willowbank Report, p. 28.

[36]Byang H. Kato, "The Gospel, Cultural Context and Religious Syncretism," Let the Earth Hear His Voice, pp. 1216-28.

[37]Ibid., p. 1223.

[38]S. J. Samartha, ed., Faith in the Midst of Faiths: Reflections on Dialogue in Community, (Geneva: WCC, 1977), p. 148.

[39]Ibid., p. 149.

[40]Kato, p. 1220.

[41]For an excellent study on syncretism, see W. A. Visser't Hooft, No Other Name (London: SCM, 1963).

[42]Ariarajah, p. 9.

[43]Mahatma Gandhi, Young India, 11 Aug. 1927, cited in The Message of Jesus Christ (Bombay: Bharatiya Vidya Bhavan, 1963), p. 38.

[44]Mahatma Gandhi, Harijan, 17 Apr. 1937, ibid., p. 73.

[45]Raymond Panikkar, The Unknown Christ of Hinduism (London: Darton Longman and Todd, 1964).

[46]Harry Sawyerr, Comments on "Is There More Than One Way to Do Therapy," Gospel in Context, I (1978), pp. 34-35.

[47]See Robin Boyd, An Introduction to Indian Christian Theology (Madras: CLS, 1969 and 1975); Horst, Bürkle and Wolfgang M. W. Roth, eds., Indian Voices in Today's Theological Debate (Madras: CLS, 1972) (English edition); S. J. Samartha, The Hindu Response to the Unbound Christ (Madras: CLS, 1974).

[48]Boyd (1975), p. 69.

[49]A. J. Appasamy, My Theological Quest (Bangalore: Christian Institute for Study of Religion and Society, 1964).

[50]It has been frequently noted that Chenchiah's thinking preceded or paralleled that of Teilhard de Chardin.

[51]Bruce J. Nicholls, "Nairobi 1975: A Crisis of Faith for the WCC, Themelios, 1 (1975), 66-75.

[52]"The Authority of the Bible" The Louvain Report in The Ecumenical Review (October 1971), p. 434.

[53]Ibid., p. 426.

[54]Ibid., p. 427.

[55]Ibid., p. 428.

[56]Ibid., p. 431.

[57]Ibid., p. 435.

[58]Andrew Kirk, "The Use of the Bible in Interpreting Salvation Today: An Evangelical Perspective," *Evangelical Review of Theology*, 1 (1977), 12-14.

[59]See A. C. Thiselton, "The New Hermeneutic," *New Testament Interpretation*, ed. Howard Marshall (Exeter: Paternoster Press, 1977), pp. 323-29.

[60]James Packer, "Hermeneutics and Biblical Authority," *Themelios*, 1 (1975), 4.

[61]For these and other examples see *W. A. Wisser't Hooft, 62-68.

[62]See René Padilla, "Hermeneutics in Culture," *Gospel and Culture*, Bermuda, 1978 (to be published).

[63]For a recent evangelical discussion, see A. C. Thiselton, "Understanding God's Word Today," *Obeying Christ in a Changing World*, ed. John R. W. Stott (London: Collins, 1977), I, 90-120.

[64]Cited in *New Testament Interpretation*, p. 313.

[65]See Sawyerr, pp. 34-35.

[66]Klaas Runia, "The Trinitarian Nature of God as Creator and Man's Authentic Relationship with Him: The Christian Worldview," *Let the Earth Hear His Voice*, p. 1009. In this chapter I am indebted to Dr. Runia's excellent paper at several points.

[67]See Leslie Newbigin, *The Relevance of Trinitarian Doctrine for Today's Mission* (London: Edinburgh House Press, 1963).

[68]Runia, p. 1019.

[69]George David, *The Eclipse and Rediscovery of Person* (Bombay: TRACI, 1976). See also *TRACI/ETS Journal* (April 1978), pp. 43-50.

[70]Runia, p. 1020.

[71]Runia, p. 1011.

[72]*The Willowbank Report*, pp. 31-32.

[73]Mbiti, pp. 31-32.

[74]Ibid., pp. 31-34.

[75]Ibid., p. 36.

[76]J. Andrew Kirk, *Gospel in Context*, I (1978), p. 25.

[77]*The Willowbank Report*, pp. 17-18.

[78]See M. M. Thomas, *Salvation and Humanisation* (Bangalore: CLS, 1971).

[79]*The Willowbank Report*, p. 26.

[55]Ibid., p. 428.

[56]Ibid., p. 431.

[57]Ibid., p. 435.

[58]Andrew Kirk, "The Use of the Bible in Interpreting Salvation Today: An Evangelical Perspective," Evangelical Review of Theology, 1 (1977), 12-14.

[59]See A. C. Thiselton, "The New Hermeneutic," New Testament Interpretation, ed. Howard Marshall (Exeter: Paternoster Press, 1977), pp. 323-29.

[60]James Packer, "Hermeneutics and Biblical Authority," Themelios, 1 (1975), 4.

[61]For these and other examples see W. A. Wisser't Hooft, 62-68.

[62]See René Padilla, "Hermeneutics in Culture," Gospel and Culture, Bermuda, 1978 (to be published).

[63]For a recent evangelical discussion, see A. C. Thiselton, "Understanding God's Word Today," Obeying Christ in a Changing World, ed. John R. W. Stott (London: Collins, 1977), I, 90-120.

[64]Cited in New Testament Interpretation, p. 313.

[65]See Sawyerr, pp. 34-35.

[66]Klaas Runia, "The Trinitarian Nature of God as Creator and Man's Authentic Relationship with Him: The Christian Worldview," Let the Earth Hear His Voice, p. 1009. In this chapter I am indebted to Dr. Runia's excellent paper at several points.

[67]See Leslie Newbigin, The Relevance of Trinitarian Doctrine for Today's Mission (London: Edinburgh House Press, 1963).

[68]Runia, p. 1019.

[69]George David, The Eclipse and Rediscovery of Person (Bombay: TRACI, 1976). See also TRACI/ETS Journal (April 1978), pp. 43-50.

[70]Runia, p. 1020.

[71]Runia, p. 1011.

[72]The Willowbank Report, pp. 31-32.

[73]Mbiti, pp. 31-32.

[74]Ibid., pp. 31-34.

[75]Ibid., p. 36.

[76]J. Andrew Kirk, Gospel in Context, I (1978), p. 25.

[77]The Willowbank Report, pp. 17-18.

[78]See M. M. Thomas, Salvation and Humanisation (Bangalore: CLS, 1971).

[79]The Willowbank Report, p. 26.

[55]Ibid., p. 428.

[56]Ibid., p. 431.

[57]Ibid., p. 435.

[58]Andrew Kirk, "The Use of the Bible in Interpreting Salvation Today: An Evangelical Perspective," Evangelical Review of Theology, 1 (1977), 12-14.

[59]See A. C. Thiselton, "The New Hermeneutic," New Testament Interpretation, ed. Howard Marshall (Exeter: Paternoster Press, 1977), pp. 323-29.

[60]James Packer, "Hermeneutics and Biblical Authority," Themelios, 1 (1975), 4.

[61]For these and other examples see W. A. Wisser't Hooft, 62-68.

[62]See René Padilla, "Hermeneutics in Culture," Gospel and Culture, Bermuda, 1978 (to be published).

[63]For a recent evangelical discussion, see A. C. Thiselton, "Understanding God's Word Today," Obeying Christ in a Changing World, ed. John R. W. Stott (London: Collins, 1977), I, 90-120.

[64]Cited in New Testament Interpretation, p. 313.

[65]See Sawyerr, pp. 34-35.

[66]Klaas Runia, "The Trinitarian Nature of God as Creator and Man's Authentic Relationship with Him: The Christian Worldview," Let the Earth Hear His Voice, p. 1009. In this chapter I am indebted to Dr. Runia's excellent paper at several points.

[67]See Leslie Newbigin, The Relevance of Trinitarian Doctrine for Today's Mission (London: Edinburgh House Press, 1963).

[68]Runia, p. 1019.

[69]George David, The Eclipse and Rediscovery of Person (Bombay: TRACI, 1976). See also TRACI/ETS Journal (April 1978), pp. 43-50.

[70]Runia, p. 1020.

[71]Runia, p. 1011.

[72]The Willowbank Report, pp. 31-32.

[73]Mbiti, pp. 31-32.

[74]Ibid., pp. 31-34.

[75]Ibid., p. 36.

[76]J. Andrew Kirk, Gospel in Context, I (1978), p. 25.

[77]The Willowbank Report, pp. 17-18.

[78]See M. M. Thomas, Salvation and Humanisation (Bangalore: CLS, 1971).

[79]The Willowbank Report, p. 26.

CPSIA information can be obtained
at www.ICGtesting.com
Printed in the USA
LVHW091545170919
631360LV00002B/446/P